Kwanzaa and Me

By the same author

Kwanzaa and Me

A Teacher's Story

Vivian Gussin Paley

Harvard University Press
Cambridge, Massachusetts, and London, England

First Harvard University Press paperback edition, 1996

Library of Congress Cataloging-in-Publication Data

Paley, Vivian Gussin, 1929–
Kwanzaa and me: a teacher's story / Vivian Gussin Paley.
    p.   cm.
ISBN 0-674-50585-9 (acid-free paper) (cloth)
ISBN 0-674-50586-7 (pbk.)
1. Afro-American children—Education (Preschool).
2. Children of Minorities—Education (Preschool)—United States.
3. Multicultural education—United States.   4. Fantasy in children.
5. Teacher-student relationships—United States.
6. Paley, Vivian Gussin, 1929– .   I. Title.
LB1140.3.P356   1995
372.21—dc20   94-25002
CIP

Designed by Gwen Frankfeldt

To Beverly Biggs

with gratitude

Kwanzaa and Me

*T*he young black woman calls softly from the doorway. "Hey, white teacher, it's me, Ayana." Before I can turn around she is at the sink hugging me, careful not to upset the little jars I am filling with paint.

Her name is Sonya Carter, not Ayana. I called her Ayana in *White Teacher*, a book I wrote in the seventies when she was in my kindergarten, giving her the African name because she symbolized for me the excitement of this integrated school to which I had just come. Years later Sonya read that book and telephoned me late at night from her college dorm. "I'm Ayana, right?" she whispered.

Now I need her to be Ayana again, to inspire me as she did long ago. Sonya in real life, Ayana in the book, she brought a generous and loving voice to that mostly white kindergarten. "Tell me what's wrong, baby," she would murmur to a tearful classmate, and we all wanted to be the one she comforted. Say it to me, Sonya, say it to me too, was our silent plea.

I want her to tell me that this is still a good place for Ayana, this integrated classroom, because a lot of people are sure it isn't. And that it probably never was.

"Sonya, can you stay a while? The children won't be here for another half hour. I want to tell you about some things that have been happening." We sit at a low table and I try to collect my thoughts. "The thing is, I find myself increasingly inhibited on the subject of black children."

"Inhibited? You?" Sonya smiles indulgently.

"Well, that's the way it feels." I hesitate, wondering if I am speaking to Sonya or to Ayana. The memory of Ayana supports my illusions, but I am unsure about Sonya. There she sits, with dangling earrings and close-cropped hair, looking so . . . what's the word? Preoccupied? The list of grievances I'm about to unfold is not my own, but after trying to avoid them, I cannot dismiss them from my mind.

"Remember Mrs. Junius, in the high school?" I ask. "She wrote an article in which she out and out tells black parents not to send their children to this school when they are young. Or to any other white school. Especially the boys."

I wait for Sonya's reaction but she is staring at some crayon marks on the table, so I continue. "She sends her own children to a neighborhood school, an all-black school."

Sonya looks up, frowning. "It never occurred to you that we might question the integrated school?" I am mindful of her use of *we.*

"No, it didn't. This is the one thing I've taken for granted. The integrated school." Sonya shifts in her chair, glancing at her watch, and I speak a little faster.

"Then two other things happened, one shortly after the article, maybe even because of it. A middle school teacher, also black, told some people that she thinks the black boys who enter our school *after* sixth grade do better than those who begin in nursery school. In other words, they survive more intact if they spend their early years with black children and teachers."

Sonya's stoical expression confuses me. The school she has gone to is being rejected *because* it is integrated and she seems unmoved. "Okay, one more and I'm done. Last year I was on a panel with a sociology professor, the only African American in the group. He was even more emphatic, angry really, in his arguments against the integrated classroom."

My explanation must seem endless and I am grateful to be nearing the end. "He announced that he wouldn't send his little girl to a white school, no matter how good it was supposed to be. He said, 'I won't have her coming home from school telling me she's dumb and ugly. My friends' kids have had this done to them.'"

"So have I, Mrs. Paley," Sonya says quietly. "Plenty of times."

"But your mother never told me."

"Well, maybe not in kindergarten. Probably back then I imagined myself a blond blue-eyed Cinderella. But later, when I stopped pretending . . . Listen, this sociology professor and the others, they know what they're talking about."

I am annoyed with myself for suddenly remembering a doll-corner scene in which she imagined herself a *black* Cinderella. Or was it someone else who had used "black" with such confidence? "But, Sonya, he wants his daughter in a segregated school! The kind he himself *had* to go to before desegregation."

"Ah, so this is why you don't write about the black children any more," Sonya breaks in.

"Should I?" I ask. "Just what is their school experience? Here are some very thoughtful people, yourself included, who are so certain it's a bad one I'm almost afraid to tackle the subject." I reach across the table and take Sonya's hand. "Did you really feel dumb and ugly?"

Sonya is so solemn I think she might cry. "I was walking on eggs the whole time. Hell, I still am. All these places I've been sent to are racist. They can't help it. My mom hates when I talk this way to a white person. Oh, did she tell you I'm transferring to Spelman? I've wanted to go to a black college for a long time but I worried about my folks. Turns out they don't mind a bit."

We listen to the sound of children calling to one another in the hallway. Then Sonya gets up, swinging her backpack into place. "And so you sidestep the whole business by writing a book about everyone being nice to everyone without exactly mentioning to whom. And the black folks go into those Magpie stories of yours where you can control matters a bit."

Sonya is referring to my most recent book, *You Can't Say You Can't Play,* the story of a classroom experiment in which children are no longer allowed to reject one another, hence the title. To lighten the load I have added a magical bird named Magpie who accomplishes similar ends with a variety of lost and lonely characters, some of whom are black.

"They *are* nice stories, by the way. How did you ever think of including them in such a serious book for grown-ups?" Before I can answer, Sonya grabs a brown crayon and steps to the easel, drawing three brown-faced people with crowns on their Afros. "Let's see, there's Princess Annabella, Prince Kareem, and Maruska the doll—they look black but they sure don't talk black!" She gives her words an exaggerated drawl and laughs.

"Would you like to know why I made the princess black?" I ask. "There were three black girls who ignored a black doll I'd

4

just bought. They played with a white doll that wasn't nearly as pretty. So I named the black doll Princess Annabella and made up a story about an African princess who lives with her father in a lonely forest . . ."

Sonya raises her finger. "Until Magpie brings them to the Kingdom of Tall Pines. Yeah, how come you never sent a magical bird to rescue me?"

"Funny thing," I answer sadly, "when I wrote *your* book I didn't think you needed to be rescued. *I* was the one floundering in self-doubts."

Sonya sits down again. "Did it work?" she asks. "Did they play with the black doll?"

"Yes they really did. And they also began to draw brown faces." I point to her sketches. "They'd never done that before at school. The effect was remarkable."

Sonya smiles at me. "Not strange at all. See, you create the characters in your Magpie stories and the child whose real story is touched upon feels legitimated." She jumps up and walks around the table. "That black doll now *belongs* in this classroom. She's been given a name and an important story. That's it! We black kids need a story of our own inside the classroom story. I think you're onto something. By the way, has Magpie met any more black folks?"

"Well, yes, as a matter of fact. I brought in a new character just yesterday, in a chapter about a runaway slave named Kwanzaa."

Sonya whoops with laughter. "Fantastic! Kwanzaa? My secret holiday is your runaway slave?"

"But, Sonya, why has it been such a secret? I just discovered Kwanzaa last week."

Sonya stands over me, her brows arched, her head held high.

I remember that look. She is my Princess Annabella, for sure. "Because never once," she measures out each word, "did any of you teachers mention Kwanzaa. It was in the newspapers but you were not the least bit curious. We knew we'd sound ridiculous if we talked about it."

"Why ridiculous?"

"It was too *black,* too African sounding, too pushy. It didn't belong here, which meant *we* didn't belong here. But no one said stuff like that then."

We stare at each other. Then Sonya gives an apologetic smile. "Please don't feel bad when I tell you this. I really do agree with that professor. I'd have done better in a black school. I'd have been more confident. I was an outsider here."

*I*t is Lorraine Barnes, one of our third-grade teachers, who tells me about Kwanzaa. Passing her room a few days before Sonya's visit, I notice what seems to be an odd-looking Chanukah menorah on her desk.

"There *is* a menorah over there on the window sill, but this is a kinara," she explains. "See? Seven branches. We use it to celebrate Kwanzaa." With no sign of recognition from me she adds, "That's an African American holiday. It comes right after Christmas."

"But I've never heard of it!" I exclaim.

"It's not very old," she replies kindly. "It began in the sixties and our family took it up immediately, my uncles especially. They've always been big on anything that brings the black community together."

As Lorraine speaks I try to remember if she had ever mentioned "the black community" when we taught together in the same classroom fifteen years earlier. Why had she not told me then about Kwanzaa, I wonder.

"The purpose of Kwanzaa," she continues, "is to honor and practice the virtues that strengthen family and community, things like unity, industry, creativity, and so forth. I can give you something to read if you want to know more. By the way, not every black family celebrates Kwanzaa."

After reading the pamphlet I call Kesha's mother, figuring, perhaps unrealistically, that a family giving their child an African name probably celebrates Kwanzaa. Mrs. Johnston sounds surprised and pleased when I ask her to teach us about Kwanzaa. "My pleasure," she says.

"I'll come tomorrow if I may. There's nothing you need to do. I'll bring everything."

Kesha and her mother arrive wearing matching blouses of an African design and carrying covered baskets. The smaller basket holds a shiny red wooden kinara and a straw mat on which to place it, and the larger one bears fruit and corn, colorful scarves and shawls and wood carvings, along with red, black, and green candles and other objects. In it are also teacakes still warm from the oven. "My mother-in-law's recipe," Mrs. Johnston says. "She's our Kwanzaa expert. She's even learning to speak Swahili."

Kesha lifts one item at a time while her mother explains its meaning, always in personal terms. "This is Kesha's daddy's favorite," she says, pointing to a silver goblet. "We sip from it to show that we are one family. Then we eat the fruit of the harvest and we thank those who planted and harvested the food. Can you say 'chakula'? That's the Swahili word for food." The children practice the new word while Mrs. Johnston arranges the remaining objects on a second straw mat and puts the candles in the kinara. "Kesha's grandparents brought these hand-carved animals home from a trip to Africa, and the scarves and shawls too. Kesha, honey, shall we put on the shawls and sing our Kwanzaa song?"

At this point, with everyone staring at her and several children giggling, Kesha loses her nerve. Undaunted and smiling, Mrs. Johnston puts both arms around her daughter and sings out: "Kwanzaa is the time to celebrate, The fruits of our labor, Ain't it great! Celebrate Kwanzaa, Kwanzaa!" By the second repetition, many of us are singing along while the teacakes are passed around.

Then Mrs. Johnston reads to us from a book of African folktales, about Anansi the spider who is saved from many disasters by his brave children. To reward them he throws a dazzling sphere of light he has found in the forest high into the sky to become the moon for all to enjoy, and everyone dances. "Ngoma," she tells us. "Ngoma means dancing to the beat of the drums. Now you know two Swahili words, no, three: chakula, ngoma, and guess what? Kwanzaa."

The next morning, quite unexpectedly, Kwanzaa enters a Magpie story. I am at my desk before the sun is up, looking at pictures of Martin Luther King, Jr., and Abraham Lincoln, deciding which ones to frame and bring to school. Lincoln's deep-set eyes look out from under a stovepipe hat and I know he is worried about slavery. Dr. King is pictured speaking to a large crowd and he too seems to be thinking of slavery and its aftermath. What does it mean to Kesha and the other black children to be told by me, a white teacher, that some black people had been slaves?

Suddenly I see one slave clearly and his name is Kwanzaa. He will come to live in our classroom, as have Princess Annabella and Prince Kareem, participants in the ongoing drama. I need them all to help me talk about some crucial issues: black and white, slavery and freedom, friendship, community. Children, even as young as kindergartners, are devoted to philosophical inquiry, but to go beyond the fleeting thought, they must meet these important concepts inside a story.

Am I sidestepping some problems, as Sonya suggests? Perhaps she is right. It is so easy to justify behaviors that feel good. In any case, a few of these Kwanzaa stories are included here for the same reason I tell them to the children: my journey into black and white, or to any other self-defining region, must always involve storytelling, the children's, mine, and that of all the interested parties I meet along the way.

Those pirates are in big trouble, thought Magpie, as he watched them climb out of the ship's hold. He understood their desire to escape from the king's dungeon but why steal Queen Millicent's jade chess set after she was nice enough to let them play with it? This made no sense to the large black and white bird.

He circled high above the ship until he could see the four men on deck, arguing as usual even while they fished off the bow. Only then did Magpie swoop down and go below deck to look for the jeweled chess box.

"May I help you find something?" came a low whisper. "My name is Kwanzaa."

Peering into the shadows, Magpie saw a man huddled in the corner of a tiny prison cell. "I've been so lonely sitting here," he said. "Perhaps we could talk for a while."

"I'll do more than talk," Magpie assured him, introducing himself to the dark-skinned man. "I'll try to open this rusty lock and get you out. By the way, the pirates have stolen a chess set from the queen. Have you seen it?"

Kwanzaa pointed to a trunk under the bunks. "It's in there. They expect her to pay 100 gold pieces for its return. Do you think she will?"

"Ha!" Magpie cawed. "The Royal Guards are standing by ready to sink this ship and recapture these nervy fellows." He pecked steadily at the lock, careful not to make too much noise, while Kwanzaa spoke to him of sad events. "My life is full of bad luck. No sooner do I escape from a slave owner than I am kidnapped off the ship taking me home to Africa. These pirates offered me gold to join them but I refused. I was brought up to be neither a slave nor a pirate."

The lock spring was beginning to move. In another moment or two the prisoner would be free. "How did you become a slave?" asked Magpie.

"I was digging for clams one day on the beach of my village," Kwanzaa answered, "when some men stole me away. They brought me to America in chains and sold me into slavery. I never saw my family again."

With a sharp twist of his beak, Magpie snapped open the lock. "That is a sad story, my friend, but your luck is about to change. Tell me, can you swim?"

Kwanzaa grinned and said, "I can swim like a fish and run like a deer but I cannot fly like a magpie."

"You are a brave man," Magpie said, "to be able to smile after what has happened to you. I know the king will help you return home. King Bertram is against all forms of meanness and what could be meaner than to make someone a slave?"

It is easy to get carried away when the subject is storytelling. Sonya is right in thinking I am partial to fantasy. So is she, calling herself Ayana when she comes to visit. We've had, until now, an unspoken agreement to keep our relationship on a pretend level. Her real story would have been more dramatic than the one I wrote.

And yet, this real story often emerges more forcefully when disguised as make-believe. The day after Sonya's visit, Kesha dictates a rather remarkable story for us to act out.

> Once there was a little girl in a forest. But no one else lived there. And she was very sad. So she went out to the city. But no one understood what she was saying because she was Spanish. And then she went back to her forest and sat for days and days. Until she was so tired of sitting she just went somewhere else where there was always Spanish people so they would understand her.

After school, I call Sonya and read Kesha's story to her. "That's incredible," she says. "It's as if she listened to our conversation. She's black, right? That could have been my story only I don't speak Spanish."

"She *is* black, but couldn't it have been anyone's story?" I say. "And she doesn't speak Spanish either. Actually the story puzzles me because Kesha seems to be a confident, happy, very sociable girl." Just as I remember Sonya herself.

We are silent for a moment and I hear laughter in the background. "Am I interrupting something?"

"It's okay," Sonya assures me. "The relatives flock over when I'm home from school. But, this story. Isn't it unusual for a kindergartner to be so expressive?"

"Kesha's story is unusual, I agree with you. But they can all tell pretty good stories when given a chance. I hope I listened to yours in kindergarten. I hadn't started keeping them yet and we didn't act them out either."

"Did you do that with Kesha's story?"

"Yes. She took the part of the Spanish girl and the rest of us first pretended to be the people who didn't understand her and then, at the end, we were the people who *did* understand her. It was better than any adult treatment of the subject of isolation and community you could imagine."

"Speaking of community," Sonya says, "I do remember playing in the doll corner with a lot of black girls. Did we really have that many when I was in your class?"

"That year we had eight or ten black children in the class, as I recall. Last year we had only three and this year there are four. Times have changed."

"Why is that, do you think?" Sonya asks.

"Maybe for some of the reasons you yourself have given. Perhaps that's where the explanation for Kesha's story lies: there are not enough black children here."

12

Walking through the halls of our school, I have color on my mind. The children who scramble past come in nearly every shade of the birches, pines, and wind-swept dunes of my summers. They are the colors of the chipmunk and trout, the deer and the gull. In point of fact, however, most of the girls and boys are white.

We are a large private school on an urban university campus, an integrated island, both school and neighborhood, within the predominantly black South Side of Chicago. Our school is approximately 65 percent white, 15 percent black, and 10 percent Asian. Perhaps 2 percent of the students are Hispanic and the rest call themselves "other."

Nearly 80 percent of the teachers are white. It is the sort of place the sociology professor does not want for his child. All the colors of woodland and beach do not disguise the attitudes, sounds, and rhythms of our school: it is white. If the professor sat in my classroom, even if he liked my ways with children, he would see the absence of color. More important, perhaps, he would worry about the behavioral monotones of a middle-class white teacher.

"I don't want my baby spending all her time trying to figure out what a white teacher wants her to be," the professor had said. I think I know what he means. As a Jewish child in the Chicago public schools I struggled to fit the mold set by my non-Jewish teachers.

Like Sonya keeping Kwanzaa "secret," I carefully guarded Rosh Hashanah and Yom Kippur along with a few other holidays. The Jewish children stayed home on those days but no teacher ever mentioned the reason for our absence. We understood that we were not to speak of it, that it would sound "too Jewish."

Have the African American children in my classes already learned not to act "too black"? We have books about black children on our shelves and pictures of black heroes on the wall but both Sonya and the professor would say these are not enough. We need more people and curricula that are black. They are right, of course. But I will still be white.

Call me brown," Kesha had said to me during the first month of school.

"All right," I replied. "And what will you call me?"

"I can call you peach. With spots." She examined my hands. "What are they?"

"Some people call them age spots. I'm getting older."

"What do you call them?" Kesha wondered.

"I guess I don't call them anything. Just spots would be fine."

"Okay, peach with spots for you and brown without spots for me, except this one and this one on my cheek."

Jeremy and Martha are playing Guess Who? It is a twenty-question type of game in which one player attempts to identify his opponent's card by eliminating the other possibilities.

"Does your person have a mustache?" asks Jeremy, who is black, of Martha, who is white. "No mustache," Martha responds, and Jeremy places face down on his board all the mustached faces.

"Does your person wear a hat?"

"No hat." Down go the cards with hats.

"Is the person white?" is Jeremy's next question. Martha is puzzled. "What do you mean?" she wants to know. Jeremy repeats his question. "White. Is it white? The person, is he white?"

Martha turns to Annie, who has just arrived. "Jeremy says white. Is it?" she asks, and Annie looks doubtful. The card in question reveals a pink-cheeked, yellow-haired girl, but neither white child knows the girl is called white.

Seventeen of the twenty faces in the game are white, as are eighteen of the twenty-five children in our class, plus two white teachers. Jeremy sits in a sea of white faces yet his question is not understood. I am reminded of the time I said "gentile" in front of my second-grade teacher and she snapped at me, "You mean Christian!" My face was hot with confusion and embarrassment. I had thought Christian was the word we weren't supposed to say.

I call to Kesha, who is coloring at a nearby table. "Come see if there are any white faces in this game, will you?" She stares at me.

"They're all of them white," she answers, walking over to the game. "Except for just this one, and this, and this isn't." Kesha watches Martha with interest. "Aren't you white?" she asks her. "You look white."

"I'm pink," Martha responds. She is six years old, bright as can be, and she doesn't know she belongs to what we call the white race. It wouldn't matter except for the fact that Jeremy and Kesha and Rasheem and Ashley, our four black children, *do* have that information and we all live together in the same classroom. Later, when I describe the scene to Jeremy's father, he thinks it's funny. "I'm not surprised," he says. "White kids don't have to know that."

Nor white teachers, it seems. When I introduce my Magpie characters, I specifically refer to the brown skin and African origins of Princess Annabella, Prince Kareem, and Kwanzaa. I do not feel I must explain that everyone else is white. Princess Alexandra, the king and queen, Corporal Thomas and his son Raymond, and all the others apparently do not require racial identities. They simply *are*.

However, now the secret is out and I'll have to talk about it. After the game, I call everyone to the rug next to the piano where most of our discussions are held, and I bring the black and white dolls with me.

"Annabella is black," I begin, holding up each doll in turn, "and Alexandra is white. If Princess Annabella lived in America she would also be called African American. Or brown. Kesha calls herself brown. And Mrs. Barnes sometimes says she is a person of color. Now, Martha calls herself pink and Kesha once said I was peach with spots. Jeremy's mom calls us Caucasian. And Maria's dad says 'Anglo.' But most people would call me, Martha, Princess Alexandra, and a whole lot of people in this room white." Why am I doing this in such a clumsy way? It would have been better simply to describe the Guess Who? incident and let the children involved explain what happened, as I usually handle such events. Obviously the subject is an awkward one for me.

"What color is Magpie?" Rasheem asks.

Bless you, my child. Magpie to the rescue. Again. "He's black and white, with a bit of shiny green and blue showing when he spreads his tail." Everyone looks up at the colorful display of children's drawings on the wall, of magpies, brown and white princesses, and red-headed Raymonds. The orange flower people are there from a past series of stories and so is Kwanzaa, the newest member of the picture gallery. He is darkest of all, sitting in a boat, getting ready for the trip home to Africa.

"I'm not a color," says Vijay, who is from India. Jeremy leans over to ask, "Would you like to be light brown?" Vijay nods, satisfied.

If I am to increase my understanding of the vulnerability of the African American child in a white majority, then who better to speak to if not the black parents in my own classroom? Why have they chosen our school? What are their hopes and fears? Do they too believe we are a racist institution?

I invite Mrs. Johnston to come in first, probably because she responded so quickly to my Kwanzaa request. Kesha's brother and sister have been here for a few years and the family is active in school affairs.

"I'll get to the point," I tell Kesha's mother. "A young college friend of mine who used to be in this kindergarten thinks our school is racist. I've heard that other black people feel the same way."

Mrs. Johnston is quiet for a moment as if judging my intentions. Then her words flow easily. "Black families talk about this all the time. There are some that at one time sent children here or to other white schools who no longer do, for just this reason. Although economics may have something to do with it too.

Anyway, I'll have to agree with your friend. It's a subtle institutional racism but it goes back to people. I think it begins with the teachers. Children don't care; they just want someone to play with. But, at some level, every teacher brings her biases into the classroom. Kesha and her sister and brother come to school with a good spirit. My husband and I seek out teachers at every grade who are able to promote the good spirit of every child."

"But aren't you describing good teaching in general? How does racism enter the picture?"

"To me racism is more about people wanting to be in control. More than you're black and I'm white, you're Jewish and I'm Christian. It's about people not letting my children have a say. Sure, white children are hurt too, but African American children are more vulnerable than any other group. They feel different right from the start and they worry about it."

"Is color the main difference?"

"Yes, but nearly everything seems different. Kesha comes from a preschool that has no white people. The talk is different, the style, the subject matter even. That's okay, because black children should have a deep grounding in their own sense of self before the age of five or six. They must know early on that their history and culture have as much merit as anyone else's. Then they can go into any environment and not get shut down."

I describe to Mrs. Johnston the professor's concerns as well as those of my black colleagues. "They think black children *will* get shut down here," I say.

Mrs. Johnston nods. "People in my family feel the same way. But I don't agree. Something can go on in a white school to support this special spirit. It can be done by white teachers. I've seen it happen with my children."

"Is it more likely to happen in an all-black school?" I ask. "This is what I want to understand."

"Not necessarily," she states with emphasis. "Okay, I need to explain something. School becomes a large part of a child's life, but it is only a part. If there are no other pieces you're going to have a big gap, even in a good black school. For us, there is our church, our homes, here and in North Carolina, plus all the roles and experiences we bring. Kesha has seen role models in African American women in every activity."

"Can white people be role models?"

"You bet," she smiles, "as long as they respect and encourage my children to express their differences, their particular culture and knowledge."

"Then you're not concerned about integrated schools," I conclude.

"We deliberately sought one out. Look, our church is African American, so is our family, so is our neighborhood. This is Kesha's first exposure to white people. It's not too soon. We think it's important for black kids, all kids, as early as possible to be exposed to a multicultural environment."

She looks over at the cubby area as if trying to find a name. "And not only whites. Kesha talks about a boy from India. Vijay? She wants to know why does his mother dress that way, why does she have a dot on her forehead, are they brown or white? There is so much to find out about people. You can't start too early."

I decide to show Kesha's Spanish girl story to her mother. "Read this, will you?" I say. "And tell me what you think it means."

Mrs. Johnston studies the story carefully, reading it three times. "Such tender feelings my girl has. I'm impressed. What do I think it means? That she misses her friends from preschool. Her black friends."

*B*efore she leaves, Mrs. Johnston urges me to talk to Jeremy's parents. "They have a great many doubts about this school." I call the Arnolds and Mr. Arnold agrees to meet at seven the next morning so he can be in his classroom by eight. He teaches math in a high school less than a mile away.

"We're still pretty ambivalent," he says when I repeat Mrs. Johnston's comment. "My wife especially. She'd like Jeremy to remain in an African American school until he's older. But I know the public schools better than she does. I teach in one. Jeremy would get into trouble because he's curious, argumentative, questioning everything, like me. They don't like that in the public schools. They want obedience. He'd be labeled bad immediately. This has already happened in preschool."

"You expect more leeway here?"

"Oh, definitely. But even so, I worry. People say to us, why send him to a white school? He'll get blamed for everything. That's the perception. Six boys run wild and the black kid is punished first."

The word "racism" hasn't been mentioned. Something tells

me Mr. Arnold won't say it unless I do. "Is it a matter of racism?" I ask.

"Yes, it is, a subtle, intellectual racism. It's because white people don't feel comfortable and can't interpret things going on with an African American kid. Not only him, of course, but I know there is less tolerance for black cultural differences. There are always these indirect put-downs, especially for the boys."

"Like what?"

"White boys are seen more often as smarter, better prepared for school. There are lower expectations for black boys. It's very subtle, these put-downs," he insists. "Let me explain something. There are differences in parenting and socialization in my culture that are not put into context by white teachers. The African American culture is different in style and substance and those differences are seen negatively. Okay, here's an example: We are a very religious family and quite Afrocentric. Our kids know a lot about the Bible and certain religious ideas we believe in. Certain heroes are important to us. When my nephew—he's in the fourth grade—talks or writes about these things, the teachers think we're fanatics. They don't say it but my brother is sure of it." He smiles. "We wouldn't be in this school if we were fanatics."

Mr. Arnold stands and removes his jacket, pointing to the window. "Mind if I open it?" While he does I think about what he has just said. It makes sense. In a school such as ours we are quick to think that religion-spouting children, black or white, come from nonintellectual backgrounds, whereas a child who constantly talks about, let's say, outer space exploration might be considered bright. "Mr. Arnold, are you saying that this problem would not exist in a black classroom?" I ask when he resumes his seat.

"No, it wouldn't. Even if the teacher were an atheist, she'd fully understand the cultural context of these ideas. She would consider it *information*, not inappropriate parroting." He stands up again and walks around, stretching his legs and arms. "Plus there's the language problem. We know standard English. But if our kids revert to home-talk while they socialize the teachers think less of them. Any use of colloquial black speech, style, or substance creates a negative impression."

He returns to the table with a bigger chair. "Furthermore," he says, "it's across the board. When I attend professional meetings, of math teachers and the like, whites and Asians are listened to with more respect than African Americans. Okay, I can handle this. But I don't want my kids to be put down."

I look at him without speaking for a moment. "And yet Jeremy is here," I say.

"Right. And so I'm going to watch carefully and participate as much as I can." He glances around the room. "By the way, who is this Kwanzaa? Should I know him?"

I laugh. "No, I made him up entirely. I'm a storyteller, it's part of my teaching. I only recently discovered the holiday and gave the name to a character in a continuing story I tell. He has just escaped from slavery, been kidnapped by pirates, and saved by a magical bird. So far." I bring over Jeremy's notebook, flipping the pages until I find a recent dictation. "Your son tells stories too. Read this, you'll enjoy it."

Mr. Arnold skims over the story and then reads it aloud.

Once there was a black Michael Jordan and a white Michael Jordan and the black Michael Jordan got the most points but the white Michael Jordan got the most rebounds. So then they were friends and they played together every day.

His eyes are wet. "Sorry, I'm an emotional guy. This is wonderful. It's why I want him to go here. He's got to be comfortable with whites because I'm not. I got a late start. In high school there were a few, but when I got to a white college I nearly flunked out. Culture shock." He reads Jeremy's story again and chuckles. "Say, you want me to come in and tell a story? I also like to tell stories."

"I don't want Kwanzaa to leave us," Princess Annabella complained one morning as she got ready for school. "Can't he stay here always?"

The prince knew how his daughter felt. "I'll miss him too, my child. He reminds me of my cousins in Africa. But you know he must return to his family. Imagine how worried they are."

"You don't understand, father. When he's gone we'll be the only African family again." Then Annabella remembered something that made her smile. "Guess what Kwanzaa told me when he picked up a pine cone? He said it was the color of the children in his village."

Prince Kareem had come from just such a village. "I hope he'll return one day soon and bring his family with him. Meanwhile we have good friends here. Alexandra and Raymond love you as a sister. And Schoolmistress thinks of you as her own child. It doesn't matter that we are black and they are white."

Annabella kissed her father goodbye and started for school. Alexandra stood waiting for her at the edge of the forest. "Are you sad?" Alexandra asked when she saw her friend.

"You see, I've become so fond of Kwanzaa," Annabella explained. "The ship he and Corporal Thomas are building is nearly half finished. I'll miss him when he leaves us."

Alexandra took her hand. "Would you be sad if I went away?" she asked.

Annabella hugged her friend. "Oh yes, I would. Let's always be friends, promise?"

And Alexandra promised.

A few days later, Mr. Arnold brings Jeremy to school and stays long enough to tell us a story. "Once when I was little," he begins, "Martin Luther King, Jr., came to speak at our church. It was a long speech and I don't remember most of it, but there was something he told us about his daughter Yolanda that I never forgot. Jeremy's already heard this but he says he doesn't mind hearing it again."

He smiles at his son and goes on. "When Yolanda was young, her daddy was always being invited everywhere to give speeches. And she liked going in the car with him to the airport. They always drove past a big amusement park. I think it was called Playland."

"Or maybe it was Great America," Martha suggests.

"Like that only much smaller," he says. "Everything was smaller in those days. There were no big malls or Great Americas. So this was a small park but the rides seemed wonderful to Yolanda. Every time they drove by she asked her father if he would take

24

her there when he came back from his trip. And when she asked him he looked very uncomfortable and said, 'Yolanda, honey, I'll try my best,' but he never took her."

"Well, this happened again and again and one day Yolanda burst out crying and she couldn't stop, she was that unhappy. They had been on their way home from the airport and she knew there was time to go on the rides. She was still crying when they got home."

The room is absolutely still as he continues. "Her daddy realized he had to tell her the truth. So he sat her on his lap and said, 'Yolanda, honey, there *is* a reason your mother and I can't take you to Playland. And it's a very mean reason because it makes a little girl like you cry.' Yolanda looked at her father with her big dark eyes and asked, 'What's the reason, daddy?'"

"'They won't let you go on the rides because you're black. Those rides are only for white children. I hadn't wanted to tell you this.'"

"Yolanda wasn't crying any more. She was trying to figure out what her father meant. Finally she said, 'Then I don't like those rides.'"

"Dr. King hugged his daughter and smiled at her. 'It's okay to like those rides, honey, and it's okay to want to go on them. Those people are wrong, not you. But baby, listen to me. Even if you can't go to Playland, you're just as good as all the children who can go. Not one of those kids is nicer or better than you!'"

The children are still quiet as Mr. Arnold finishes his story. Then Jeremy stands up directly in front of his father. "Can Yolanda go on those rides now, daddy?" he asks.

Mr. Arnold lifts Jeremy to his lap. "She's a grown woman now. She can take her children there whenever she wants to."

"Hey, guess what? They can go to Great America, too," adds Rasheem helpfully. "We might even have my birthday there."

I go once again to Lorraine Barnes's room, this time to tell her about Yolanda and the amusement park. She has already heard the story but I repeat it anyway. The choice of this particular story by an African American father who worries that his son may be "put down" in our school has a powerful effect on me. I feel I can speak freely to Lorraine of these matters because, in my mind, she lives in both camps. I quickly discover that I have underestimated the changes taking place in the black community.

Lorraine is one of a few black teachers in our lower school. She has taught here for more than fifteen years and, besides, both of her children went to our school, from kindergarten through senior high. She is, I am certain, the living affirmation of my belief in this integrated school. However, when I tell her about the sociology professor, I see that Lorraine herself is full of questions and doubts.

"I've heard that sentiment about black children being in black schools," she responds, without emotion. "It's similar to what people say about women in all-women's schools, that you really do have your own voice, that people are not constantly measuring you against another standard. Yes, people do have the feeling that in a black school every gift a black child brings will be valued, that black children will be more valued in a black school."

Lorraine's words are not what I wanted to hear, yet I sense that she can give me the context I need to step back and listen in a new way to what black people are saying. "Can we talk frankly, Lorraine? Can we meet regularly and go over some of the things you've been learning?"

She laughs, a deep-throated laugh that always makes me want to join in. "Hold on, don't pass me off as an expert," she says. "Because I'm not. I have been thinking a lot more about these issues than I used to, that's true. Sure, I'd like to talk. Maybe this will help me get some things out in the open."

Thus begins a series of conversations that will continue throughout the winter and for most of the spring. During this time, I will pursue my questions and concerns with others as well, with teachers who visit our school from distant places and with people I seek out when I'm invited to their city to speak. But always, everything will enter the crucible of the ongoing dialogue with Lorraine and the parents of my students.

The biggest surprise for me is the effect of the stories the parents tell, not only the black parents but all the parents. Except for the children's own stories, it will be their parents' memories that most make us feel part of the same community.

Rasheem's mother has come to tell us a story. Mrs. Stocker is known to all the children, for she often stays a while when she brings her son in the morning. "Rasheem told me to come with a story today," she says, "so here I am. He's heard this before, but not the part at the end. That might surprise him. Now, let's see. When I was young, maybe a little older than you, we lived in Mississippi. Every Sunday after church we all went to my grandparents' farm for dinner. Then they'd give us bushels of corn and peas and beans, things like that, and when we got back home the whole family would sit together and bag the vegetables. It was a big job. So, anyway, here I am, sitting on one side with my brothers and sisters, and my parents on the other side, and we're all shelling black-eyed peas."

"What are they?" Edward asks.

"They come in a green pod, honey, a shell really. You open it up and there's a whole row of peas, each one with a black dot, like an eye, sitting there, just waiting to be put in a pot. But I'm in a bad mood. I want to go out and play. Why do we have to sit here and shell peas? I don't even like peas. So I begin to cry and everyone looks at me. Now, of course, I had to keep shelling. In those days, you did not disobey the grown-ups. But I keep grumbling and sniffling.

"Suddenly, my dad starts looking at the floor and talking to me in a sad voice. He said, 'When I grew up we just barely had enough to eat. Some nights you'd go to bed without eating at all.' Now this was the first time I realized what my dad's life was like when he was little. 'Papa, how could you be hungry if you lived on a farm and grew things to eat?' That's what I asked him.

"'Oh yeah,' he said, 'we had a whole lot of crops but they weren't ours. See, we did something called sharecropping. You work the soil and grow all the food but you have to give it to the person who owns the land and even owns the house you live in.'"

Mrs. Stocker's gaze travels from child to child. "Boys and girls," she says slowly, "my father and his family had all this food but they couldn't eat it. My father got up when it was still dark to work all day but the food he grew was not his to eat."

Rasheem moves closer to his mother. "But when did grandpa go to school?" he asks, worried.

"That's just it, honey. Your grandpa couldn't go to school. When he was a kid he had to go out every day and pick cotton and plant corn. That's what your grandpa was telling us that time when I didn't want to stay inside and bag the vegetables."

Now Mrs. Stocker looks directly at Rasheem. "This is the part you don't know, son. And I hadn't known it until that moment when he told us. He said, 'I know how important it is for you to go to school because I can't read.'"

Rasheem is surprised. "Grandpa didn't learn how to read?"

"No, he didn't. And while he sat there telling us, a tear was coming down his face. Well, I stopped my complaining right there and then. You'd never hear me arguing about something I had to do, because we had lots of good food and I was able to go to school."

"But what did your father eat?" Jennifer asks. "Did he starve?"

"Well, no, they could keep whatever the owners didn't want. Maybe some of the beans and vegetables didn't look good or were spoiled. And they also had something called ashcake. They would put cornmeal inside the ashes in the furnace, cover it up until it got a crust on top, and when it's done, there's cornbread inside. Pa said that's mostly what they ate."

Jeremy raises his hand. "Guess what, Mrs. Stocker? Your father didn't need to cry. Abraham Lincoln's father couldn't read either."

"Oh, is that so?" asks Mrs. Stocker gently. "Who told you that?"

"Kwanzaa told us, right, teacher? Didn't he tell us that the other time?"

"I was luckier than most slaves," Kwanzaa told the children as they sanded the oak boards he and Raymond's father were hammering in place to make the deck of the ship. "An older slave named Jamal taught me to read. That helped me to escape because I could read maps and road signs. And newspapers too."

Corporal Thomas stopped hammering so he could listen to Kwanzaa. He enjoyed the time he spent showing the young African how to build a seaworthy vessel, and Kwanzaa, in turn, was teaching Raymond and his father how to carve animals out of soft pine. Best of all, however, the corporal liked to hear Kwanzaa talk about himself. So did the children.

"Did you go to a school like ours?" Annabella asked.

"Oh, no," he said. "There were no schools for slaves. We worked in the fields from sunup to sundown picking cotton. Jamal read to me from a book called the Bible every chance we had until finally I could read the words for myself. Abraham Lincoln learned to read in the same way. His mother was his teacher since his father couldn't read."

"Who is Abraham Lincoln?" the children asked.

Kwanzaa had forgotten that children don't usually know who the leaders are in faraway lands. "He is the ruler of that country, the president, they call him. And he hates slavery. He once said, 'As I would not be a slave, I would not own a slave.' I read that in a newspaper."

"Then why does he allow it?" demanded Alexandra. "My father would never permit slavery in our kingdom. Never!"

Corporal Thomas and Kwanzaa sat down to rest. "Your father has more power than Mr. Lincoln does, Alexandra," Kwanzaa replied. "In America, people vote to elect leaders and to make laws.

It takes a long time to change a bad law if a lot of people don't want it changed. But President Lincoln has promised he will free the slaves and I believe him."

Raymond settled down beside Kwanzaa, his pale skin looking even whiter next to his dark friend. "You never told us how you escaped," he said. "Was it real scary?"

"Oh, yes, scary and dangerous," Kwanzaa answered, "but some of us managed to escape, with the help of good folks, black and white both. People like Harriet Tubman. She had been a slave herself and after she escaped she kept helping others get away."

Kwanzaa picked up his tools and began to work again. "When we have more time," he said, "I'll tell you all about the Underground Railroad, not a real railroad, but a route to freedom, from house to house, village to town, across river and stream, until you were safe."

Annabella tried to imagine what it must feel like to be a slave who was running away. She had always been free to come and go as she wished. She didn't think she could be as brave as Harriet Tubman. "How did she know what to do," Annabella asked, "since she was also a slave?"

Kwanzaa smiled at the young princess. "I've wondered about that too," he said. "There must be some people who want so much to help others they find a way. Harriet Tubman led hundreds of slaves to freedom. She must have been scared too but it didn't stop her. What a true friend she was. I called her 'rafiki.' That means friend in my language."

"Did you ever worry that your own children were not valued enough in this school?" I ask Lorraine at our first "official" meeting. The Barnes children had not been in my class but whenever I saw them they seemed confident and happy.

"My kids did well, for the most part, but I could mention others who were not so fortunate. Look, this concept of black kids in a black school is not unlike the way I feel about raising my kids in a black neighborhood. Where we live the sense of community has always been great, with neighbors of all ages who care about us. It would be very different in a mixed neighborhood like this one where people tend to keep to themselves. It reflects in our school, I think. Sure, our community won't be the world my children will have when they move away but at least they'll be operating from a real base of strength."

Kesha's mother had described her community in the same way, a place that nourishes spirit and soul, she said. Lorraine uses other words but it comes out sounding the same. "Everyone in our neighborhood knows everyone. My children have been watched and talked to and worried over and have been a source of pride to the entire community. I can appreciate what this professor of yours is saying, about raising his child in a black school. People do know why so many of our leaders came out of black schools like Morehouse, Howard, Spelman, and the others."

"There was a time," she continues, "when I wouldn't have felt this way. I would have said, definitely you must be in an integrated setting. I still think it was right for my kids because they were protected by a large family unit within the extended family, neighborhood, and church. But I do understand now why more people are thinking about all-black schools."

Lorraine seems to be saying that the integrated school could be dangerous for the unprotected black child. "So then," I comment, "if you come from a strong family and community it's safe to attend this school, but if there's a breakdown of support you'll need a black school? Forgive me if this sounds preachy, but didn't you and I tell each other long ago that the classroom should be a family with all sorts of people learning to care about each other and respect each other's differences?"

Lorraine does not disagree. "But that can go on in a black classroom too. Look, why can't it all work? All black, all white, all girls, all boys, or integrated in dozens of different ways. Why do we have to decide one is better than the other? We have to be not so judgmental about the choices."

We look at each other a bit warily, and then at the clock. It is time to stop.

$\mathcal{T}$here are times I think I should return to a black school," Lorraine says as we begin our next conversation. "I started out teaching that way. It was all black, maybe one or two white teachers. The principal was white, so rigid, someone who'd been in the system too long. She didn't have a clue about what black children were like. There was no relationship."

"About what *any* children were like," I ask, "or just black children?"

"We had good reason to believe black was the issue. I remember a teacher doing Black History month in the hall, putting up a display and being told to take it down. This was in 1966. 'That's better kept in the classroom,' she was told. But it wasn't unusual in public schools—yes, even black public schools—in those days to find a self-consciousness that thank heavens is no longer there."

"Did you leave because of the principal?"

"Oh no, she wasn't very important to me. I loved it there. It was a wonderful place for a young black teacher, and I was only twenty-one. Most of the teachers were the age I am now. They took me under their wing, showed me how to do things. There is a feeling of community in a black school I've never seen anywhere else. It's a feeling of kinship. I miss that. Don't get me wrong. Here there is a real feeling of mutual respect, but it's not kinship and it has nothing to do with color."

But maybe it does have something to do with being black. Sonya brought that feeling into our classroom and since then other black children have done the same thing. Janet Albright, a black student teacher I once had, helped create this family feeling. I tried to analyze her method, giving her, in fact, a chapter to herself in *White Teacher,* yet I don't think I understood that being black was an essential ingredient in her obvious talent for kinship.

Lorraine continues. "Frankly, I *am* wondering if I should stay here, at an integrated school. And believe me, this school is much more aware of and appreciative of black culture and black children than it used to be. I see it with so many teachers and administrators. So it's not just that it's integrated. But it's so *privileged.* I didn't come from a privileged background. I'm not the only one who says this. White teachers say it too."

There *are* many affluent families here. But there are also many who struggle to pay the tuition and there are families who receive scholarship aid. I point this out to Lorraine. "We're not that exclusive. Come on, you know how many people borrow and scrimp and save to send their children here."

"Oh, I agree fully," Lorraine replies quickly. "I'm talking about *poor* people. And there are too few people of color. Vivian, I can't tell you what happens when I go to this educational conference of people of color." Lorraine is excited now. "I've been to it twice. What an instant sense of community there is!"

Lorraine explains that this is a yearly meeting of private school teachers who come together to discuss what they give to their schools and what the schools give to them. "There are African Americans and Asians, Hispanics, Native Americans. There is almost always this instant rapport, this instant community. There are so many shared concerns. You see, most of us teach in predominantly white private schools. But we sense community in each other. It's hard to explain. I have good friends in this school, people I treasure, and there isn't a classroom I've gone into where I'm not warmly received. But it's not the same feeling I'd have at a black school."

Suddenly I have a sense of loss. There are so many things I must discuss with Lorraine. I feel like Princess Annabella contemplating Kwanzaa's departure. "You mustn't go, Lorraine. We need you here." She gives me a gracious smile but I can tell her mind is filled with thoughts of going home again.

*T*he next weekend I am in a small Pennsylvania town to talk about children's play and storytelling. Afterward a young black woman named Karen approaches me. "I like your use of Kwanzaa," she says, "but I'm sorry you would have a former slave speak well of Abraham Lincoln. He should not be a hero to African Americans."

"Can you tell me why you feel this way?" I ask.

"Because he didn't care a bit if slavery continued. He said if he could keep the union together without freeing a single slave he would." She frowns. "You must know this."

"Yes, but he also said, 'If slavery is not wrong, then nothing is wrong.' There are dozens more places where Lincoln spoke or wrote of his hatred of slavery." I wait for her reply.

"He's your hero, not mine," she states firmly. "His birthday is not easy for me, but of course I have no choice. My school is almost entirely white. You must have seen that in the audience today."

There are only two black children in her fourth-grade class, she tells me. "Neither one has a strong sense of heritage so it's up to me to provide this. I've discussed it with my principal, all of my feelings. He says as long as I don't knock Lincoln and Washington I can add any other heroes I like. So I do. This year there's a Mexican child and I'll talk about Zapata and Pancho Villa."

"How do you handle Lincoln?" I ask, remembering a school I taught in, before desegregation, in the Deep South, where I was cautioned to skip over Lincoln. "We don't pay him much notice here," I was told.

"Oh, he's still Honest Abe and all that," Karen says, "but I also tell the children he was more about keeping the union together than about slavery. And when we talk about Washington, I mention that he was a great general and he refused to be a king, but he did keep slaves. I'll bring in Crispus Attucks and Harriet Tubman and Nat Turner—and Malcolm X too."

We continue talking as she walks me back to my hotel room. "What sort of school did you attend when you were young?" I ask.

"I'm from your town, Chicago, South Side. I hardly ever saw a white person until high school, then not too many. We'll move back when my husband gets his degree, or maybe to Detroit, where his family lives. In any case, it will be to a large African American community. And we'll put down roots. My mother thinks this place depresses me, hardly having any blacks here. She says I used to be more joyful."

"Maybe she's right," I say. "You'll feel freer to be yourself. Although your principal is an understanding man, isn't he?"

Karen smiles. "I'd love to take him with me, red hair and all. He'd be a stand-out where I'm going."

As we begin our goodbyes, Karen poses a different sort of question. "How does your new rule work? 'You can't say you can't play'? I've been thinking of using it. The kids can really be mean to each other. It was the same when I went to school. No difference between black and white there, I'll tell you."

This is rather nice, I muse. Karen and I begin with our differences concerning Abraham Lincoln and end up discussing exclusionary behavior, a problem common to all classrooms.

*M*onday morning. Kesha, Barbara, and Gracie have run out of the doll corner to complain about Michael, Edward, and Jeremy. It is girls versus boys, this much is clear.

"They wreck our house down," Kesha claims, "because they're jealous of how we make it. They just don't have the *courage* to ask us to play because they think we're going to say no."

"I wonder why the boys think you're going to say no," I propose.

Jeremy pushes through. "Oh, sure, they know why. See, they keep covering up everything with blankets so we can't see what they're doing. They say it's private. I told them no private allowed. So they just covered up some more. So we had to pull off the covers to see what was there."

The girls are incensed. "We are not saying you-can't-say-you-can't-play!" Kesha explains. The rule, posted above the piano, is often referred to this way, as if it is one word. "We're just saying it to the boys. All the girls can play."

"We want to be separate," Barbara adds, "like Martin Luther King."

Jeremy laughs and claps his hands. "Oh, boy! He said *don't* be separate!"

Barbara sticks out her tongue. "I mean don't be separate *girls*, so there!"

This is becoming complicated. I ask Jeremy, "When your father came to talk about Dr. King and Yolanda, did he say anything about boys and girls being separated?"

Jeremy gives my question serious attention. "Well, Daddy wasn't reminding himself of that."

"Right. Your father remembered the time Yolanda King couldn't go to Playland because she was black. We'll ask Daddy to come back and tell us how Martin Luther King felt about girls telling boys they can't play. Or boys telling girls they can't play, which

I definitely have heard on the playground before. That should make a good discussion for us."

*L*orraine is grinning when I next enter her classroom. "I've got a story for you," she says. "I read a book to the children this morning that had the word 'Negro' in it and a boy asked me, 'What's Negro?'"

"These changes come fast," I marvel.

"Very fast," Lorraine agrees. "So I wrote on the board: Colored, Negro, Black, African American, and Person of Color. I told the children, 'Over time, what we have been called and what we call ourselves has changed. When Harriet Tubman was alive, people were called coloreds, then later Negroes. Kids will ask me what I like and I tell them I like black and African American. Here's why I like black so much: before the sixties many thought black was not beautiful, black was ugly. Black hair, black skin, black noses. We couldn't even call each other black without it being an insult.'"

I ask Lorraine if black had the same impact then as "nigger" and her reply amazes me. "No, indeed. Unless it's used by a white person, nigger is not a bad term for blacks to use with each other. *I* don't say it because I don't like the word, but blacks will use that word as a term of endearment."

I cannot hide my surprise. "Lorraine, I always thought 'nigger' was like 'kike,' an insult no matter who uses it. I'm glad you explained this to me. I have in the past stopped black boys in the hallway from saying this to each other. It hasn't happened often but it has happened. Would anyone in your family use the term?"

"Not in my immediate family. But in my extended family? All the time."

"How is it used?" I ask.

"Somebody will say, 'Hey, nigger, how you doin'?' Just like that. I grew up hearing that word bandied about. Not in my house. My father wasn't comfortable with it. In my mother's family they were. Not, of course, if a white person was around."

I'm still thinking about the boys in the hallway. "Lorraine, you're in a class with black and white children. A black child calls another black child 'nigger' and a white child gasps, 'Oh, what he said! I'm telling!' What do you do?"

She has a quick answer. "It's happened. I'd just say, black people sometimes call each other by that name. It's okay for them but not for whites."

This seems wrong to me. "So then the white child says, 'I don't get it. How can that be okay for them but not for me?'"

Lorraine does not see this as a problem. "It's a piece of social knowledge kids have to learn. I can see this bothers you."

"I guess it does. Look, when Kenny said 'shit,' I told him not to, and he argued that his parents both say it. So I told him they wouldn't say it in a classroom. It's not polite. Why isn't 'nigger' in the same category? Now, you taught in a black school. Would that term have been used?"

"Not often, no. The child would realize that certain words you can use at home but not in school, as you said."

"But wouldn't you tell the child that?"

"No, Vivian, I really wouldn't." This is said almost as if she thinks I am being purposely obtuse, but I must pursue the matter. "Would you be surprised to hear a teacher use the term in a black classroom?" I ask.

"Yes. In a classroom. There are ways we talk among ourselves, all of us, that we don't talk among the larger society. It's called code switching."

"Okay, so shouldn't that black child in your class be code switching by third grade? How come *he* doesn't have this social knowledge? And since he doesn't, shouldn't you be giving it to him? Or I? Can't we tell him it makes white people uncomfortable, all the more so since we are not allowed to say it."

Lorraine is adamant. "No, I wouldn't say it makes someone uncomfortable. I'd just say, if it came to that, this is a word that's appropriate to use at home and outside school, but not in school."

I want to return to the sociology professor's concerns. "Do you think it takes too much out of a black child to learn what is acceptable to a white teacher?"

"Of course not. Now listen, all these people you've been talking to are middle class, just as you and I are. They already share most of the values of this school. I think a lot of this has to do with class, not race. Anyway, kids are pretty smart, no matter where they come from. They've already figured out what they can say at church, at grandma's, in the family, on the playground, and certainly they're finding out what they can get away with in school. There are always different expectations from different people and you learn to act accordingly."

Walking home I find myself still wondering about the black boys in the hallway. What will I say the next time I hear someone call his pal "nigger"? I can't ignore it since I *am* present, within hearing distance, and therefore it is no longer private. Might I say, "Boys, I know that word is okay between the two of you, but it's not appropriate in school in front of a teacher. So would you mind saving it for when you're alone?" That sounds acceptable to me. I walk home much relieved, yet with the nagging feeling that I had stumbled into the "nigger" issue before but without a resolution I could understand.

*T*he next day I remember that once long ago a student teacher in my class told a black child not to say "nigger." "Say it at home if your folks do," she said, "but they most definitely do not want you saying it in school." I wanted to ask what she meant by "say it at home if your folks do" but something stopped me. Twenty years later I have the conversation with Lorraine I should have had then with Janet Albright.

Janet and I did have other talks about black and white, however. "I'm not cut out to be the 'company black,'" she told me when I urged her to stay and teach at our school. "If I'm as good as you say, let those who need me have me." Furthermore, she suggested that I do the same, come with her to a black inner-city school.

As I think about these events now, a new memory floods my consciousness, an unwanted memory. The reason I did not go with Janet then is virtually the same as the one that worries the professor now: I did not want to feel a stranger in a culture not my own. Am I expecting young black children today to do something that I, as an adult, lacked the courage to do twenty years ago? But times are surely changing. Two decades ago I was unable to come right out and ask a colleague why a black family would use the word "nigger" at home, but now I can comfortably argue its usage with Lorraine. Are these genuine changes or merely superficial intellectual exchanges?

A few years after Janet left our school, we had a second-grade opening. I called her, and again she declined. "We're putting our language arts program on more of a black culture foundation," she told me. "It's pretty interesting and I'm learning a lot."

"You sound happy."

"I guess you've caught me on a good day" was her response. "The public schools are really pathetic. We get fewer and fewer resources all the time. My school has no music or art teacher this year and our supplies are in terrible shape. The school is filthy and the playground is full of broken glass." Then she burst out laughing. "Hey, listen to me. Call me in ten years. Maybe then I'll be ready to leave."

Over the years, Janet and I have continued to call each other, usually on our birthdays, which are a week apart, and always we keep the banter light and gossipy. Now she is on my mind again. I call her as soon as I get home from school.

"Hey, remember? You told me to call in ten years," I say when she comes to the phone. "We've got a first-grade opening next September that practically has your name on the door."

Janet laughs warmly. "I appreciate the thought, I really do. But I must be honest. I just wouldn't be happy in a white school."

"Is it because you think it's racist? I've been hearing this more and more lately."

There is no ambivalence in her response. "The whole society

43

is racist. How else to explain what's happening in the housing projects these kids come from? If these were white neighborhoods would the criminals and madmen be allowed to take over?"

"You have a right to be angry," I say.

"Aren't you angry?" Her question is sharp and my response is quick. "Yes, I am, and I'm also ashamed that these terrible things are allowed to happen."

There is a moment of silence and then Janet's voice becomes warm and inviting. "Listen, I wish you could see these kids, Vivian. They are so eager to learn. When school is over they don't want to leave. I'm teaching a first and second grade and we're creating such a rich African American environment. We've got neighborhood artists and performers coming in and parents volunteering to do story dictation or help with the reading and writing. They even come in to help us clean up."

"Janet, I'd like to visit. May I?"

After a barely perceptible pause, she replies. "I wouldn't if I were you. We've had some bad things happen in the neighborhood. A little girl was shot on her way to school. A stray bullet."

"Oh, Janet! I'm so sorry. What a tragedy!" We talk for a while about the child and her family and then we say our goodbyes, promising to meet when, she says, things settle down.

All the next day I can think of little else but Janet and the slain child. When Mrs. Johnston comes to pick up Kesha I talk to her about it. "How awful," she murmurs. "My husband and I can't stop talking about these tragedies. Sometimes they are people we know or relatives of people we know. And yet, our pastor is right: the rest of us must keep our anger but also must keep going and act as if the world *will* turn around and right itself one day."

She bends down to tie Kesha's shoe, then looks up. "But I'll tell you one thing. The barrier to this school is not race, it's economics. We should, all of us, find ways to bring more African American children here who can't afford to come. Not just here, but to all the good schools in safe places. This should be our first priority right now."

$\mathcal{M}$rs. Johnston arrives unexpectedly the next morning to tell us a story. It is as if she must remind herself and all of us that there was a time when simple happy events occurred regularly in a child's life.

"When I was little I was pretty lucky," she begins. "My mother took my brother and me to school with her every day. She owned a little nursery school and kindergarten in North Carolina and she was our teacher too. Wouldn't you like that? To have your mother for your teacher?"

Most of the children nod approvingly but Jeremy is not sure. "Did she spank you?" he asks.

Mrs. Johnston laughs. "No, we were all pretty good. What I remember best was our playground. It was on a high place, on the edge of a cliff. If you were real careful and looked over and down, there was a river, a beautiful, fast-flowing river. We had two swings in our playground and if someone gave you a good push you could swing high, high almost to the sky."

"And touch the clouds," Ashley adds.

"Not quite, honey, but it did feel like you were swinging over the river. You couldn't really get across because there was a big fence there but you felt just like a bird flying back and forth over the river."

Mrs. Johnston's story prompts a flurry of phone calls from other parents offering to come in with their own childhood memories. Nearly every child in the class, it seems, has brought home the image of Kesha's mother swinging over the river. Vijay's father asks to come in the next day because he is leaving soon for a business trip and does not wish to disappoint his son.

"I was born in a small village near Calcutta in India," he tells the class. "We had a sliver of a stream that ran along between our village and the forest. From the moment our summer holidays began, all the children played in the stream. We built dams out of stones to make the water tumble faster and we sailed pieces of wood, pretending they were ships on the ocean. One day my cousin Kishore screamed that he saw a bear in the woods and we all ran home. Then he said it was a joke and we were all angry with him. However, we didn't want to waste time being angry because soon it would be time to return to school. And so, every day, if our mothers wanted to find us, they knew we would be playing in the stream."

We stare at Mr. Shah as if we have never seen him before. Then we look at Vijay, our shy Vijay, and he is grinning. "There!" his smile seems to be saying. "Now you see how much there is to know about me."

"Oh, Annabella, Alexandra! Is it time for school already?" School-mistress asked. The girls had not expected to find their teacher sitting under the apple tree with Kwanzaa. She was reading him a letter and showing him a picture of a young girl.

"*I've had some sad news,*" Schoolmistress said, "*and also some exciting news. The sad part is that a good friend from childhood has died after a long illness. But there is something else in this letter that will change my life forever. My friend's child is coming to live with me.*"

"*Can't her father take care of her?*" wondered Annabella, whose own mother had also died.

"*I'm afraid not,*" answered Schoolmistress. "*He was lost at sea long ago in a storm. No, Kavitha is an orphan. Would you like to see her picture?*" The girls were surprised to see a girl of their own age dressed in silky scarves from head to toe. "*Annabella,*" whispered Alexandra, "*Kavitha is almost as dark as you. Isn't she pretty?*"

Schoolmistress stood up. "*What worries me,*" she said, "*is that Kavitha is an Indian child and I know very little about India. I don't know how the people from her land live and talk and do things. I'm afraid I shall seem very strange to the poor child.*"

Kwanzaa remembered how he had felt the first time he met a white person, a sailor who had been washed ashore near his village. He was almost afraid to talk to the stranger. But the man turned out to be much like Kwanzaa's own father and they became good friends. "*Yes, Schoolmistress,*" he said, "*you may seem strange to Kavitha at first, but soon she will learn your ways and you will learn hers. The main thing is that she knows you love her and are happy she has come.*"

Annabella put her arms around Schoolmistress. "*You will make her happy, the way you make us happy,*" she said. "*And we'll be her friends, won't we, Alexandra? I've never met anyone from India before.*"

Alexandra squeezed her friend's hand. "*And maybe she's never met anyone from Africa. Or from the Kingdom of Tall Pines.*"

47

*T*oday we have a visitor from Lebanon. The children ask if she is Indian because she wears a head covering and I have just described Kavitha swathed in her silk scarves and sari as she arrives in the Kingdom of Tall Pines. Majida's gray headdress, simple and sedate, is more like a nun's.

She has come to study American schools and work toward a doctorate. Lorraine would call her a person of color, though she is no darker than I am. Later, Majida will tell me color is of no importance in her native land. In any case, she has the look and sound of an outsider, and it is this feeling I want to probe. After a suitable interval, during which several children drape themselves in scarves and come to sit with her, I ask Majida if she will return after school to talk about multicultural education, in her country and in America. She seems eager to do so.

As we speak together I realize that the universality of school life makes it possible for us all to understand each other's experiences and expectations. This is true even when, as in Majida's case, war and political strife have disrupted the general pattern of life.

"My school was composed of both Moslems and Christians but we were all Arabs," she begins. "Before 1975, the beginning of the war, children didn't really understand which religion they belonged to. Anyone who could afford to send their children to Catholic school did so because it provided a better education."

"Did you, as a Moslem, feel different, being in a school where another religion was followed?" I ask.

"No, not at the beginning. We had math, we had science, we had religion. They were all school subjects, having no connection

48

to my daily life once I went home. In any case, nothing we heard at school was strange to us. You see, Islam is a continuation of Christianity and Judaism. We believe in everything in the Old Testament and the new Bible."

"But you are taught to say these things in other ways," I comment, "and perform other rituals."

"Yes, but, you see, the situation in Lebanon at that time was nonreligious. It was more about political parties. Everyone who had an opinion had a party: Communism, Socialism, Nationalism, Right, Left. There was not then a call for Islamic rights or let's go back to foundations. Everybody was trying to be on an equal basis with everyone else."

"Did it work?"

"No, that's why we have war. It never worked. Before the war, children never talked about religion. When the war started, they began to ask each other in school, Are you Moslem? Are you Christian? As if one day you woke up and everything changed."

"Were you taken out of the Christian school then?"

"All my village was ousted. We went to Beirut." Majida tells her story in such calm tones it takes me a moment to understand what she has just said. "All my village was ousted." This sounds so frightening, but before I can find out how it happened, she has returned to the time before the war.

"I mentioned that everyone spoke Arabic. But with our French teachers we all spoke French. This was not to demean our language but so we would learn French very well, which we all wanted to do. It was not easy to tell us apart, Moslem from Christian. Most names could be either one. My name is a Moslem name. And in Islam, girls usually begin to wear head scarves at nine, though I didn't until I was sixteen. The country was at war and religious issues started to show up more."

"Majida, did you feel then, when you were ousted, like an outsider in your own country?"

"I don't think in terms of being an outsider but there have been feelings of unfairness for a long time. The Christian villages have better schools and hospitals. The Moslems are increasing, some say we are 70 percent now. But we still don't have good schools, good hospitals, good social work, or government jobs. That was part of the beginning of the war. People were dissatisfied, not because they belonged to a certain religion per se. It was a matter of political parties. It is not, as in America, a matter of race," she points out.

"It surprised me when I first came here, two years ago, the extent to which race is discussed. In Lebanon, I would never look at the color of my neighbors. It's not a standard we use. Maybe how much money, how much education, what religion, but not the color.

"You ask me, Vivian, about feeling like an outsider. Here, in your country, I get the feelings of outsiders and insiders. I think the black community feels sometimes like outsiders. Perhaps it has to do with the idea of being brought here by force. The history of slavery makes them feel different. But at the state university I went to last year, all the international group, people like myself, we all seemed to fit in with the black students. We discussed things. We had commonalities. By the way, the teachers were very sensitive. They went out of their way to ask minority students for their ideas and opinions. I like it when people ask me about myself."

50

At this point, I describe some of the concerns of African Americans about the fate of young black children in an integrated school. I ask Majida if she herself would seek an Islamic community and school if she lived in America and had children.

Majida tells me she thinks about this often. "I would be as concerned as these black parents. The identity issue. Our religion is not easy. There are many deep attachments that must be learned at an early age. But if the children attend a school where their identity is accepted and the teacher tries always to help them belong to the larger group, explaining their differences when necessary, then the integrated school could be a good thing. Without a power structure built in, transferred to a child through his peers, it might work. Children raised here should have the advantage of not having the same problems as their parents. If I keep my child in an Islamic school, I could be re-creating the problem of being an outsider all over again."

Yes, she makes a crucial point: this power structure is implicit in the curriculum and in the teacher's behavior, and is then transferred to a child through his peers. Mrs. Johnston put it another way: "It's about people wanting to be in control . . . not letting my children have a say."

"I think I know how black people feel," Majida says. "They're starting with the assumption there is a certain difference, in their case, color, in mine, religion. The struggle is to find out how to deal with these differences between ourselves and the mainstream. At what age can the child explain what she believes in even though it is different from what everybody else believes, and still feel okay about it?"

"It's something I wonder about," she continues. "Shall I wait until my child has built a self-concept, at eight, nine, or ten? Or is it better to start with other children from early childhood? For blacks, as for me, there is a cultural heritage that would not be present in the school community or in the communication patterns of teachers. Here is a black child who loves his parents. But he goes to a school where so much of who his parents are means very little. And he carries it in his color, maybe in his speech, every moment. My child carries it in her observances and in her manner of dressing."

"Then what is the answer? How will you decide?"

Majida adjusts her scarf and stands up to leave. "I shall find out if the parents are part of the school. This is what would decide me. I don't want my child confused by being part of two strands. But if I see that teachers reach out to me and my family and want to include us, then I would choose the integrated school. I would want my children to feel they belong to the mainstream American culture."

$\mathcal{M}$ajida's color-blind society is of great interest to Lorraine. "This is something even we blacks do to each other," she tells me. "We'll discriminate against each other on the basis of color. Light is better than dark. I remember this from my childhood. I was one of the darkest in my family and, although this was not an issue in our family, I could see that for some people it was."

"I haven't noticed this attitude among the black children in my classes," I comment.

"There is actually less of it in this school," Lorraine agrees. "I think the kids are used to so many shades of color that the subject diminishes in importance. Also, when we are thrown into the broader culture we look for the things that unite us."

What an agreeable notion this is, a definite plus for the integrated school. "Hey, anything that lessens the importance of color, I'm in favor of," I say. "Tell me more good things."

Lorraine laughs. "Are you keeping score? Okay, here's one for the other side. Well, maybe not. We'll see when I'm finished. There is a way most black teachers will look at black children that most white teachers can't manage to do. Take, for example, the subject of hair. A minor topic, you think? A black teacher knows that *hair* can and does create big problems. I'm thinking of Courtney right now because you had her in kindergarten but I could mention many others."

Lorraine shows me the class picture, pointing to Courtney, whose hair is piled high into an elaborate topknot. "One of the big issues with Courtney is her appearance, her hair in particular," she notes. "It's a big issue with many in the black race, period. She has in her hair a relaxer that straightens her hair. It's obvious that her mother sets her hair every evening and Courtney comes to school with a nice hairdo every day. But let's say her hair gets mussed up in the rain and now it's all frizzy. Then another black girl might make a big thing out of it: 'Oh, Courtney, what happened to your hair?' Courtney feels terrible, is in a terrible mood, and it affects everything she does all day."

Remembering Courtney, I am certain I paid too little attention to her hair. "And so," I suggest, "a white teacher might be impatient and think, well it's only hair, this is only third grade, don't make such a fuss, Courtney." Would I really be so insensitive or am I playing devil's advocate? "Okay, so what does a black teacher do?" I ask.

"For one thing, I'd step in and give a quick lesson on black hair. I'd say, one of the things we black people might do is straighten our hair. And if it gets wet it curls up again. That could happen to my hair too because my hair is straightened. Now I tell this to all the children, not just the black girls."

It seems to me this is a good example of Majida's requirement for the integrated classroom, that the teacher explain each child's differences when necessary. I tell Lorraine of Majida's expectation and she agrees enthusiastically. "Absolutely. That's the point. The teacher should be able to explain, *when necessary*. For this, she needs *information*. Now, continuing with the hair issue, sometimes a fourth-grade black girl doesn't want to go swimming because her hair will be horrible looking, she thinks. Even with swim caps, some water gets in. So she makes a big fuss and everyone is annoyed with her. Again, it's a serious problem."

"Okay, so I have all this information," I say, "but the girls still have to go swimming. Then what?"

Lorraine is eager to explain. "Then I call the parents. 'Look,' I say, 'you want your child to benefit from the whole program in this school, don't you? Style her hair in a way that makes it easy for her to manage.' I tell them about my own daughter when she was in the fourth grade, that she had the same problem, and we did thus and so."

I am beginning to see the dimensions of the problem. "So if I called it might come across as criticism? From you it's a helpful hint, from me it's a put-down?"

"It doesn't have to be," Lorraine says. "The more information you have the better you can handle this problem. I'll bring you a magazine I read where this whole phenomenon of hair is discussed. The author points out that we black women take our hair so seriously. Some people decide that the way you wear your hair is a political statement, that anyone who straightens her hair is denying her cultural heritage. And don't even think about coloring it! If you cut it short, wear a wig, braid it—everything you do is a political declaration."

"I take it then that you and the author don't go along with this," I say.

"It's absurd" is Lorraine's reply. "But, getting back to the classroom: Once I had a girl, Tiffany, who had very short hair. Her mother styled her hair in little braids. That allows the hair to grow and not break off. One day, Tiffany wrote a story in which she said, 'I got a blond hair today.' I asked her what it meant and she showed me her collection of hairs. She kept them in a tissue: blond hair, red, black, brown—but all of them *straight* hairs from her white classmates. They knew all about her collection and would pull out a hair and give it to her. I realized something had to be done. I made no mention of the hair collection but I did make a point of telling her often how nice her hair looked. 'Your mom spends a lot of time on your hair,' I told her. 'Did you go to the beauty parlor?' We compared our experiences, teacher and child sharing something. I don't know if she continued to collect hair but I took this opportunity as a black teacher to let her know her own hair is beautiful."

I cannot help wondering what I might have done about Tiffany and her hair collection. I have rather kinky hair myself and could easily discuss these curly versus straight hair issues with any child. Unquestionably, Lorraine's stories are opening up a whole new world of behaviors. As if reading my mind, she offers an example of the way a white colleague of ours made use of some hair information, this time concerning a boy.

"Once Gerry admitted to me how much it annoyed her to see a certain black boy in her class wearing a pick in his hair all the time. So I told her something about the history of the pick and she repeated my story to her entire class that same day. The boy himself had never been given these facts and now a white teacher could help him understand this important part of his own heritage as well as I could."

"Here's what I told Gerry: The regular comb was not invented for black hair. The slaves always covered their hair; to try to comb it was impossible. The ordinary comb was not the appropriate instrument for this bush of hair. What was appropriate is called a pick. That is what was used in Africa. This fourth grader had been trying to preserve his identity by sticking a pick in his hair. Only he didn't have the supportive information to explain himself. A white teacher gave it to him. She did exactly what Majida would like: she explained the differences when necessary. In doing so, by the way, she herself became involved and no longer objected to his pick."

Our long conversation about hair has come to an end, but I will bring hair questions to Lorraine throughout the year, questions and stories. I think this is another plus for the integrated classroom: we are constantly called upon to explain our differences to each other. In an all-white or all-black school there is, I am certain, less likelihood that we will look for ways to explain who we are. Yet even when there is only one color in a classroom, there are as many different stories as there are people in the group. *To look for ways to explain who we are:* this would seem to be a fundamental requirement for us all in a classroom.

*L*orraine has given me a great amount of information about a subject I seldom think about in school. I could of course find opportunities to talk about Kesha's hair or Ashley's. They wear their hair in a variety of ways: ponytails, braids, natural, and straightened. There is no knowing how they will wear their hair on any given day and I have not ignored their new hairstyles. To go further than this, however, I must do as the children themselves do with new information: they put it into a story. And so shall I.

"Kwanzaa, how do the children of your village wear their hair?" Prince Kareem asked one day when he and Annabella were serving tea and teacakes to Kwanzaa, Alexandra, and Raymond. "Do they still make those tiny braids I remember so well?"

Kwanzaa smiled and said, "Ah yes, and all the girls and boys want their hair braided exactly the way the queen of the village wears hers. Now, since each queen will braid her hair according to a different design, you can always tell which village people come from by the way they wear their hair."

Annabella put down her teacup. "Can you fix my hair the way it is done in your village?" she asked. "My hair is bushy and hard to comb. I would love to wear those little braids. May I, father?"

The prince thought it was an excellent idea and soon Kwanzaa's hands were flying all about Annabella's head. He sang the song his grandmother used to sing. "Tiny braids, happy braids, a hundred to go, twist them and tie them, row by row."

"Do mine, too," begged Alexandra. "Please?"

"And mine!" Raymond joined in. "You said the boys braid their hair too. I'd like to see how it looks."

"Of course I will," promised Kwanzaa, "though it works better with thick curly hair like Annabella's and mine. But I'll do my best."

Before long, there were three sets of braids—black, blond, and bright red—bouncing about in the garden. The birds at the feeder flew to the trees to get a better view of the dancing children and Prince Kareem brought out his drums. He and Kwanzaa beat out a joyful Swahili chant: Ngoma, ngoma, ngoma, nah! Ngoma, ngoma, ngoma, nah!

Shortly after my Kwanzaa chapter, Ashley tells a hair story of her own.

Once there was a little sister and a big sister and they went to the hairdresser. And the big sister got beautiful new hair that was long curls and everything. And the little sister danced and laughed because she was happy.

That evening I call Ashley's mother. "I'll bet Tanya has a new hairdo," I say, and I read Ashley's story to her.

Mrs. Rawley laughs. "Tanya would live in that beauty parlor if we'd let her. By the way, I have a good hair story for the children. Ashley's been after me to come in, so why don't I do that tomorrow?"

Mrs. Rawley comes just before lunch and tells us of a visit to the beauty parlor and the effect it had on her grandmother's dog. "When I was around ten, every day after school I'd run to my grandmother's house so I could play with her dog, Candy. One day I stopped first at the beauty parlor to get my hair done in a real fancy style, all smooth and piled up high, because my auntie was getting married that evening. But I still wanted to play with Candy, so after the beauty parlor I went to Granny's. Well, the minute that old dog saw me he began to howl and run around the house. Either he didn't recognize me or he didn't like the way I looked. He would not come near me. The next day my mother fixed my hair the usual way and when Candy saw me he began to lick my face and climb all over me. That's how glad he was to have his pal back again."

Before Mrs. Rawley leaves, we agree to meet briefly the next morning on her way to her nursing job. I am at the sink mixing paints when she arrives but I stop immediately so we'll lose no time. "As you know," I begin, "I've been asking some black parents how they feel about this school. You're new in the community so perhaps you aren't ready to answer."

"No, I can answer now as well as anytime. We had our girls in this same kind of school in California and we would look for a similar school wherever we live. We want the best integrated school we can find. Ashley and Tanya will go to school with kids whose families expect them to go to the best colleges. We want our girls to know they are as smart as anyone else and that expectations for them are as high as they are for any white child in the school."

I point out that some black families worry about the expectations for their children in our school. "They think black children might be better off in an all-black school, at least while they are young, to be better able to deal with the racism they'll find."

Mrs. Rawley is quiet for a moment. "I quite understand those feelings. That would be some people's need and their family's need. Every member of my family has personally felt the racism out there. My father came from a very prejudiced place in Georgia and vowed never to go back. He promised himself that his six children would get the best education possible so we could live anywhere we wanted to, and he moved us to California because he'd heard it had the best free universities.

"We were very poor but my father managed, with his veteran's disability benefits, to buy a piece of land in a mostly white area. He and my brothers built a house—an unfinished one, a no-plumbing, no–bedroom doors, no-nothing kind of house—but we all lived in it and studied our lessons with him every night. We must have been an embarrassment to the neighborhood but that didn't worry my father. He did what he had to do to get us into college and we all went. Let me tell you, at that time—yes, even in California—a black person could not be a bank teller or a salesperson in a store or a schoolteacher, but my father took any kind of job he could get."

"I agree with my father," she says, gathering her belongings to leave. "The only protection from racism, imperfect though it may be, is to get the best education possible. Our girls feel at home with all sorts of people because that is the way we are raising them. We're renting an apartment near the school so that we'll have neighbors who represent the population of this school." She is almost at the door when she turns to me and says, "I know that some people make other choices. That's the way it should be."

After dinner, Mrs. Rawley calls to say that a friend from California is coming to visit. "Marla teaches in an integrated school system near Los Angeles that's managed to solve its racial problems. Ask her to tell you how when I bring her over."

Marla arrives the following week. To my surprise, she is white. "You see," I admit, "I expected you to be black because you're Mrs. Rawley's friend. This is certainly a stereotyped reaction, isn't it?"

"Sure it is," Marla agrees. "I still do plenty of that sort of thing. I started out teaching in Detroit in an all-black school, one of those well-intentioned teachers who may have always said the wrong thing and did the wrong thing out of ignorance. However, coming to California, to a diverse society, and working in a system well integrated by court order, I felt myself changing and growing."

I pour Marla some coffee and refer to Mrs. Rawley's comment about a solution to the racial problem. Marla laughs. "Solution? You bet. The people who didn't want to be integrated simply up and left. They either moved away or put their kids into private schools. We have, over the years, lost the people, mostly white, who did not want to be involved with children, uh, not of a certain color or religion and so forth, but with certain *behavior* patterns. Maybe that's just an excuse that's used. Anyway, we still had enough who remained to maintain a good balance. In my school, we are 45 percent black, 30 percent white, and 25 percent Asian and Hispanic. These families want to make it work. Whatever their racist problems, a human failing, these people want to try. It works because the parents want it to work."

"And aren't there any black families," I ask, "who prefer a black school for their children?"

"Well, now there are," Marla replies, "but at first there weren't. There is an all-black private school that opened a few years ago. I hear it's pretty good, too."

"Why do you think the school was established?" I ask.

"These are more activist black families. They feel the integrated schools don't offer enough in the way of African American culture and history. They feel it can be better done in their own school. Actually, the black caucus, in the state legislature, is very concerned that black children are coming out of public schools poorly educated. But then they go into the work force and the company is able to train them, which shows the students had the right stuff in them all the time. Why are you not educating these black children? the caucus asks. They obviously have what they need to learn."

"So what's the answer?"

"I'm not sure," Marla responds. "With all children, I think we're less sure of what we should be teaching, and the children, in general, seem less able to sit still and learn."

Annie's father brings us a bittersweet tale. It is like no one else's and it adds another necessary piece to the total classroom story.

Mr. Pattison speaks slowly. "My father was a brave soldier," he says. "He was killed in World War Two shortly after I entered kindergarten." He stops a moment as if to let us think about what he has just said. Then he continues. "When I told this to my teacher, three other children raised their hands. They said their fathers had also been killed in the war. That made us all very sad."

Now Mr. Pattison smiles at us, raising our spirits. "But then winter came and all our mothers flooded the backyards. You see, it gets so cold in Minnesota that the ice forms in December and stays solid until March. We skated every day after school and sometimes we were allowed to come out after dinner and skate some more. My father had taught me to skate before he went away. I always thought of him when I skated and I still do. He was a very fine skater."

Celia and Penelope teach together in a first- and second-grade combined class in western Canada. They have come to Chicago for a conference and are visiting our school. When they mention that the children in their class speak twelve distinct languages, I know these are teachers I must talk to, and I invite them to meet with me.

The class picture they show me includes a greater variety of skin colors and ethnic features than can be found in our entire building. There are Cambodians, Vietnamese, Koreans, Chinese, Libyans, Japanese, Ethiopians, West Indians, Poles, Yugoslavians, Native Canadians, and, like the teachers, white Canadians. All but two of the teachers in the school, I learn, are white Canadians.

"What we are," Celia explains, "more than being white, is very middle class, very Canadian-ethnocentric. We're not nearly careful enough of people's sensitivities. Here's an example: our school plans a big family potluck supper and it falls on the first day of

Ramadan, the month when Moslems fast during the day. Naturally none of the Moslem families can come. We hadn't even bothered to find out about Ramadan."

Penelope shakes her head. "Those kinds of things keep happening and we say, 'Oh, how could we have done that!' It reflects on how middle-class Canadian we are. But it isn't easy. There are all these holidays we celebrate, Christmas, Easter, Halloween, Valentine's Day, and so on, that most of our families do not observe in their native lands."

"What do you do about them?" I ask.

"The truth?" Both women laugh. "We ignore most of them. I mean we'll mention the event without really celebrating it," Celia says. "We've been trying to have the families come to do something about their own holidays. I think we're getting better at it."

Penelope's eyebrows go up. "Shall I tell her about 'O Canada'? We sing 'O Canada' every morning. Our principal pipes it into our classrooms on the loudspeaker. 'O Canada, my home and native land.' Is this meaningful to non-English-speaking children? And at assemblies we all recite the pledge, 'I salute the flag, the emblem of my country, to her I pledge my love and loyalty.' This gives Celia and me trouble, it really does. But our principal thinks these things unify us. We don't see it that way."

"How do you see it?" I ask. "What are the unifying experiences in your classroom?"

The women smile knowingly at each other. They are about to reveal the heart of their program. Something tells me it will be one of those vital pieces of information I am after. As I interview more and more people, I am convinced that the very uniqueness of each experience adds an essential element to the unexplored potential of the integrated classroom. Indeed, it is this need most teachers have to express a sense of community in individual ways that seems to generate the strengths of each classroom.

"We really are a unified classroom," Celia begins. "It comes out of the way we are together. For us, being together all day is in itself unifying. You see, *no one goes anywhere.* Our day is not fragmented. Except for gym, we integrate everything into the program ourselves: math, music, art, science, everything. We could, as others do, send the children out to a variety of special area teachers but then we might lose the thread of community life."

Penelope picks up where her partner leaves off, as if in the same breath. "We *are* a community. We don't send children out when they misbehave. If anything needs to be changed, we ask the children for their ideas. We ask them, 'How can we make our class better?'"

"But what about the language problem?" I pose this question to Celia. "How do you understand each other?"

"It's quite amazing," she replies. "Somehow, our routines, our storytelling and writing and story acting, the way we live the day always together, make us a community of people who understand each other. New children will come in without a word of English and immediately we find another kid who speaks their language and becomes their special buddy. He uses their language to communicate with the new child and English to translate back to us. The kids know they must make the connections between the new children and the teachers, and between new children and other kids. They pass on the culture. They can do this because they feel there *is* a common culture to pass on. In this, the storytelling and story acting are very important."

"Shall I tell you how we act out stories?" Penelope asks. "You see, the child stands and reads her journal. Let's say it's a Cambodian child. First she'll pick the other Cambodian kids to be in her story since she can speak to them in their common language. But then, as more children enter the story, the author and the actors have to start translating it into English and that in turn gets translated into Polish, Korean, Vietnamese, and so forth, and back into English again as various children take part in acting out the story until everyone understands most of the time. We do so many stories that everyone has the chance to understand a great deal."

"Absolutely!" Celia chimes in. "The stories are the most important unifying element. That and the discussions to solve social problems. These are the things that keep telling us we are a community."

I have a final question: "Is your school ever accused of being racist?"

Penelope answers quickly. "Here's one incident. Last year, while my son was in college, he worked in our school as a cafeteria and playground aide. He felt that two Ethiopian boys were being treated in a racist manner. He said, 'If these kids were white or even brown, but not so black, they wouldn't be singled out the way they are.' Their father tried to explain their behavior to the teachers. He said that they had come to Canada by way of Italy and this is the way boys play in Italy, roughhousing all the time. The father was sure his boys would learn to adjust to Canadian ways, but apparently the teachers thought otherwise."

"Did other boys play in the same way?" I ask.

"Sure, some did. My son insisted it was a color issue, because the Ethiopian boys were so much darker than anyone else. They were always punished first."

I ask Penelope if she agrees with her son and she nods her head.

"Despite the racial and ethnic diversity in your school . . .?"

"It's puzzling, isn't it?" Penelope replies. "All the differences in the world don't seem to alter the fact that, as we told you in the beginning, we remain a white Canadian-ethnocentric school."

Celia nods. "Our faculty needs to talk about these issues more. But it's not easy. If someone brings up something of this sort, it's quickly dropped."

*E*veryone in our class this year speaks English, and yet we seem to achieve community in the same way as Celia and Penelope's multilingual class: in the telling of our stories and the solving of our social problems. Often the two go together, as happens in Mr. Arnold's follow-up visit. He has come in during his lunch period to speak again of Martin Luther King, Jr.

"Mrs. Paley invited me back so we could talk about how Dr. King might solve a problem you're having," he tells the children. "I can't stay long because I've got a math class in an hour, so maybe someone can tell me right away what the problem is."

Martha is first to speak. "It's because the boys always think they can play with us even when they're being superheroes and we don't want that and they know we don't but they do it anyway."

"They don't even wait to see what we'll be," Michael counters. "They don't ask."

"See, sometimes we want to be separate," Kesha explains. "The superheroes are fighting people. Anyway, plenty of times the boys won't give us the blocks to use."

"Then *they* always has to tell the teacher," Rasheem complains.

Mr. Arnold repeats, in good teaching style, what each child has said and then points to the wall. "Now I notice a rule up there: 'You can't say you can't play.' Dr. King would surely like that rule. He'd probably say, 'Good going! Equal treatment. Everyone is welcome.' He might even tell you how to say welcome in Swahili. 'Karibu.' That's like saying, 'Come in and play a while.' Karibu. Then he might say, 'Well, any other good rules in this class?'"

The children call out a litany of bad behaviors: no fighting, no pushing or grabbing, you can't be nasty, don't be mean. Our discussion leader holds up his hand. "Okay. That's a list of things you shouldn't do. What are the things you should be doing instead?"

"Be nice."

"Ask people to play."

"Be polite."

"Say can you help people."

"Okay, that's plenty to get started on," Mr. Arnold says. "So, girls, if the boys follow these rules—be nice, ask people to play, be polite, say can you help people—you'd let them play?" The girls murmur their assent, a bit warily perhaps.

"And, boys, if the girls act nice, let people play, are friendly and polite, you'd let them play?"

The boys outdo each other in agreeableness. There is a chorus of "Right on!" "You got it!" and the ubiquitous "Yesss!" accompanied by raised thumbs.

"Splendid. Dr. King would approve. By the way, I remember something my own daddy once told my sister when she wouldn't let me play. He said, 'Shirley, don't you want your brother to grow up to be a good daddy? How's he going to learn to be nice to his little girls if you don't let him play?'"

"Did she let you play?" Ashley asks.

"Well, she did get better at it, but he still had to remind her now and then. Your teachers and your families will need to remind you too. And you can remind each other." Mr. Arnold gets up to leave and Jeremy runs to kiss him goodbye.

"Thanks for the story," I say. "I mean for the discussion." He turns to me and smiles. "No, it did feel more like a story."

*T*he cumulative effect of the parents' stories has begun to work its magic. By now, the children run at once to the rug when the storyteller of the day arrives. Today, Maria's mother has come to talk about her family's house in Puerto Rico.

"Our family and all our friends had houses on the side of a mountain, and each house had a room built underground, a storm room. In case of a hurricane or very bad weather, everybody would go in that room. My father told me of one particular hurricane that was very bad. This was when he was five years old. They waited a whole day in their storm room for the winds to stop howling. When they came out they saw that the house was damaged and so they fixed it. Then they went to all their neighbors' houses and helped them fix their houses. They would bring them food too. And when everybody's house was fixed they would have a big party to thank God that everyone was okay."

"Because God watches over people," Jeremy says, and Mrs. Diaz smiles at him. "We also believe in that, in our family. When a new child was born, my grandfather or my father would be so happy they would go out on their mountain and chop some wood and make a cross for the new baby." She reaches into her bag and takes out an old wooden cross. "This was made for me when I was born. I'll pass it around so you can all see it. Maria has one too, but hers is hanging on the wall in her room."

After Mrs. Diaz returns the cross to her bag, she shows us a little book written in Spanish. It is a simple tale of a puppy and a kitten who are accidently left out in a hurricane and are led to safety by a kindly mother squirrel. She reads each page, first in Spanish and then in English. I keep thinking, what a wonderful experience this is for us. Why haven't I asked other bilingual families to do this?

$\mathcal{T}$oday I want Lorraine to talk about her family and how it was for her when she was growing up in Chicago. She tells me immediately that she had a happy childhood. "My mother had two sisters and eight brothers, all living within a few blocks of us. So I had these wonderful aunts and uncles who were so good to me, always protective and funny and loving. There was time for that. We got together on holidays and it wasn't unusual on a Sunday for everyone to be at somebody's house. We all went to the same Unity Church.

"I'm the oldest of six in my family, three girls and then three boys. Ours is a close family. My father always had a job, in a factory. My mother stayed home and took care of the kids. We lived in a nice family neighborhood, here on the South Side of Chicago, not far from Comisky Park. That neighborhood no longer exists because the Dan Ryan Expressway was built right through it.

"My father's father lived with us and my mother was always there. We'd walk home from school at lunchtime and she had soup and sandwiches waiting. Then we'd walk back to school. That was the way it was. There were loads of kids in the neighborhood. They had the same kinds of families, working class, all black, and they all came home for lunch and found their moms waiting.

"Half of our teachers were black and half of them white. Such good teachers. Determined to teach us everything, and they did. They expected us to learn and we did. I remember always being encouraged to read and never feeling as if we couldn't do anything anybody else could do. Girls were encouraged to go to college but at the same time to get married and be mothers and learn to do all the things women do.

"At one point, for instance, the women in the neighborhood formed a club, a homemaking club. We met at one woman's house, Mildred's, and we learned to crochet and knit and embroider. I remember being at her house once with one of my sisters. Mildred always had a starched white tablecloth on her table. My sister was embroidering, and when she lifted her work up she had embroidered everything right on to the tablecloth. But Mildred wasn't angry. The point was we were all doing this together, teaching each other. This was back in the fifties. It was a time when mothers took their lace curtains down to the basement and stretched them out on racks. So many nice ways of doing things, and everything had to be done right.

"And there was plenty of time for play. The boys were out playing baseball every day. You could go out in front of your house and there would always be several games going on—boys and girls together, on the steps, on the sidewalks, in the street, in the corner lot. The sidewalks and streets *belonged* to the children. They were safe and inviting. We'd play Piggy and One-Two-Three O'Leary. We'd always be jumping rope, double dutch, sharing bicycles; learning new games from each other.

"There wasn't a lot of money, of course. This was a working-class neighborhood. The fathers had jobs, but they didn't usually pay well and there were so many kids. Yet there was never a sense of poverty. Not like people know poverty today. We didn't know we were poor. I know I never felt poor. I had my parents, who loved me, and there was always food and clothing."

We are suddenly aware that it has gotten dark and it is time to go home. As we walk down the stairs, Lorraine says, "There was such a feeling of community. At one point my mother got sick. I remember being very worried. But her sisters came to help and the other women in the neighborhood came to help

72

every day. My mother got her strength back, fortunately, and I never forgot this feeling of being cared for by the entire community."

When Michael's grandfather comes to tell us of his childhood in Brooklyn, I am reminded of Lorraine's neighborhood on the South Side of Chicago. Her families, of course, were black, and those on Mr. Bernstein's street were of many colors and backgrounds. However, the families were large, the mothers were at home, a grandparent or two lived with them, and the children played together safely on the sidewalks, streets, and empty lots.

"In our building," he begins, "you could hear a different language on every floor. My family spoke Yiddish, we're Jewish, and there was also Polish, German, Italian, Greek, even Chinese. In fact, the only families that spoke English were the black families, because they had been born in this country."

Mr. Bernstein looks around at the children and raises his arms. "Oh, how we played, all of us together. We played stickball and we played marbles and pinners—that's where you bounce a ball off the steps of the front stoop—and we played with our yo-yos and tops. We shared bicycles too. Not everyone could afford a bike, you know. But we were not selfish."

He asks Michael to bring him a glass of water and then he continues. "Nope, I've never seen kids who played the way we did and always on our own street. When it got dark you could hear every mother calling her own child through the open windows. 'Mikey!' 'Sybelle!' 'Myron!' That's my name. 'Bucky!' 'Norman!' All those names at the same time, ten, twelve names or more, but every kid knew his own mother's voice. And when you climbed up all those stairs, your dad would be home from work, reading the newspaper and listening to the radio. That was the way it was when I was young."

"Grandpa, tell about the marbles," Michael urges, and Mr. Bernstein chuckles. "He means that time my brother and I were arguing about who would carry the marbles upstairs. My brother pulled the bag and I pulled the bag and suddenly it broke. One hundred and twenty-five marbles went tumbling down four flights of stairs. What a noise! Every door opened and people watched while we ran around like crazy trying to find all the marbles. On every floor kids came out to help us. When we finally came upstairs again, my grandmother said, 'There! That will teach you to fight!' She always said things like that. What she meant was, that will teach you *not* to fight."

A day later we hear another marble story, this time from Howard's father. His was one of a few black families in their small Indiana town, he tells us. "It was a nice place to grow up in and I always had lots of friends." To the children's surprise and delight, his story is entirely about marbles. The class cannot get over the coincidence, and it takes Dr. Rudolph a few moments to get started. "Mr. Bernstein had a marble story!" several children call out. "Michael's grandfather played marbles too!" I am humbly reminded that it is always in the little details of life that the children find their connections to each other.

"Now that's very interesting," Dr. Rudolph says. "I'll get Howard to tell me that story tonight at dinner. My marble story took place the summer before I entered third grade. All that summer I practiced my marble game until I was the champion of my

block. I was winning marbles from everyone. My folks were not pleased because I was forgetting to do my chores, and just so I could play marbles."

"One night, after my parents and my grandparents were asleep, I snuck out of bed and decided to get my marbles and count them. I figured I could do that without turning on the light. So I got the bag of marbles off the dresser and just then our old dog, Buffy, decided to stretch himself out. He always slept in my room. Well, I tripped over him and the marbles went flying all over the room. Buffy began to howl and my grandfather ran out of his room yelling, 'Robbers! Robbers!' My folks were boiling mad at me."

"Did you get spanked?" Howard asks his father.

"Worse than that. I wasn't allowed to play marbles for a whole week and by that time there was a new champion. Guess who it was? My younger brother. But I wasn't too jealous. We were getting ready for school to start and I was beginning to think about baseball."

All the while Dr. Rudolph has been talking, I've been wondering who he reminds me of, someone I know well. Then I have a remarkable thought: Howard's father looks exactly like my image of Prince Kareem. When the doctor finishes his story, I tell him and the children of my startling discovery.

Dr. Rudolph seems pleased. "May I stay and hear one of your Magpie stories?" he asks. Fortunately, I have a new chapter ready to read.

Soon after Kavitha's arrival, she and Schoolmistress came to tea at Prince Kareem and Annabella's house, along with Alexandra, Ray-

mond, and his parents. Last of all, quite out of breath, came Kwanzaa, with Magpie close behind.

"Sorry we're late, prince," Kwanzaa gasped, waving a large square of paper. "Here it is! Magpie and I have taken all the measurements you need."

The prince studied the paper for a few moments and then turned to Schoolmistress. "Your house, dear teacher, is altogether too small, now that Kavitha has come to live with you. Don't you agree?"

Schoolmistress was puzzled. "Why, yes it is," she said. "But I can't just wish for it to be bigger, can I?"

Prince Kareem laughed. "That is exactly what you must do, wish for a larger house, and you shall have it."

"Are you speaking of some kind of magic, prince? Is Magpie's little witch friend, Beatrix, going to perform her magic? Can she do this?"

"Magic? No, hard work is more like it. We'll build a room on to your house, won't we, Kwanzaa?"

"Exactly so. WE. Everyone in the kingdom can help, and Corporal Thomas has agreed to direct the entire project. It will be just as in my village when a family needs a new house."

Schoolmistress and Kavitha were so surprised they could hardly speak. "Thank you," they whispered. But the prince jumped up. "No time to lose then! Magpie, will you fly to every cottage and spread the news? This community knows how to pitch in and help. Remember when Annabella and I first came? Schoolmistress, your house will be doubled in size in less than a week, as ours was. And when the work is done we'll have a party to thank everyone for being such good friends and neighbors."

Not everyone was happy, however. Beatrix the witch, disguised

as a moth, sat on the window sill, muttering to herself. "Oh, sure, big job, big plans, forget about old Beatrix, don't even think of asking me." She had just returned from a long visit to her mother and was feeling rather sorry for herself. "They're all paying so much attention to Kwanzaa and Kavitha, they have no time left for me. It makes me want to do something mean!"

Poor Beatrix. If she had stopped off at her underground cave she would have found Prince Kareem's invitation to tea and realized that Magpie planned to go there first to ask for her help. He wouldn't think of ignoring his dear friend Beatrix. As it was, her jealousy got the best of her and off she flew to think about what mischief she could cause.

Dr. Rudolph seems in no hurry to leave so I invite him to join us on the playground. Howard runs off to play with the others and the doctor and I sit on a bench to watch. He turns to me and says, "I'm rather relieved to know that your stories are not entirely historical or political tracts." He smiles at me. "They're just stories, aren't they? When Howard told me about a slave named Kwanzaa I was a bit worried that . . . well . . . the sadder aspects of black history would be overemphasized, as tends to happen."

"You think that's unwise?" I ask.

"Yes, I do, for children, that is," he states firmly. "I don't want Howard to think of black people as tragic figures. There's too much of that going on. Children need happy stories to make them confident. Now, we lived, as I mentioned, in a white town with just a few black families, but my folks filled our minds with happy stories. And we visited my mother's family in Alabama every summer and heard even more upbeat and funny things. We take Howard there in August so he can be with his cousins."

"But the grown-ups must be discussing these political and historical issues," I insist.

"Oh, of course we do," he responds quickly. "We are terribly unhappy at the evidence of growing racism in this country. Well, maybe not growing, but not lessening. Even so, I want Howard to hear the other side, the happy family stories. Now, here you've got my look-alike, Prince Kareem, inviting people to tea, making plans to improve Schoolmistress's house, and there's Kwanzaa, part of the organizing committee. I take it everyone else in the story is white?" he asks.

I have to think for a moment. "Well, Kavitha is a person of color, from India, and Annabella, of course, is Prince Kareem's daughter. Beatrix has been described earlier as sort of grayish. But I guess, yes, I'd have to say almost everyone is white. Do you think I ought to bring in more black characters?"

Dr. Rudolph laughs. "I don't see where it matters. Just go on telling good stories. Howard, by the way, has given us a running account of your stories. I asked him who is black and who is white and he couldn't tell me. But he knew that Kwanzaa was African. I'd say you have a well-integrated cast of characters."

"Which brings me to a quick question before we go in," I say. "Do you think our school is trying hard enough to do well as an integrated school?"

"Hmm," the doctor pauses. "That's a tough question. Well, it's certainly better integrated than the school I went to, but my wife and I think this school could do a better job of involving African American parents. You know, getting *guidance* from us

78

about matters concerning black children. That would definitely improve the school, in our opinion."

This weekend, I have come to North Carolina to speak at a statewide teachers' conference. At lunch, the first day, I ask the three women at my table to talk about their school experiences, before and after desegregation. Louise and Enid are black and Laura is white; all three grew up in North Carolina and now teach in its public schools.

Enid is the youngest in the group. "I went to an all-black school for ten years," she tells us, "and then we were desegregated. It was very painful. I come from a small town, a very close-knit black community that focused on home and church. I had to go into another world I knew nothing about. Up to then the only contacts I'd had with whites were from an occasional trip to town and with the insurance man. To have that direct contact suddenly in my junior year in high school was overwhelming. Some terrible things happened at school. But my objective was to graduate. I wasn't going to let them hamper me."

Laura is next to speak. "My school, of course, was all white. I was already in college when integration came, and when I started teaching it was at a rural elementary school just beginning to integrate. What happened was very interesting. At first, when it was still white, we had a strong PTA and a sense of ownership about the school. But after desegregation there was a lot of black and white conflict with the parents. The leadership declined and the white families moved out. When the school became black, the leadership began to build again. There was the same kind of ownership and pride. I taught there for thirteen years and saw the whole transition."

She turns to Enid and says, "I saw the sort of thing you just described when I moved to the middle school. Overwhelmed! The black kids from my former school, good students, were overwhelmed by the diversity. They were lost."

I ask Laura if the curriculum was more Afrocentric when her elementary school became black. "It really was," she replies, "though we didn't call it that. But we wanted the black kids to have more of a sense of their own history. Yet it didn't seem to make a difference once they got to the middle school. And don't forget, the whites were lost too. They didn't know how to act. They did many harmful things out of fear and ignorance."

Louise has been silent until now. "Harmful, yes. I've seen it all. I'm older than the two of you. When desegregation was ordered, I'd already been teaching in a black school for ten years. But, I'll tell you something. My father gave me some good advice when I was growing up: 'You're going to come into contact with all kinds of people. It's not your business to judge them. Just learn what you need to know to survive.' I have tried to follow his advice and I've managed to adapt to whatever my situation is."

Survival. It comes as a bit of a shock to me that our entire conversation has been about survival. Is this what defines the school experience, one's ability to survive? "What is the crucial factor in this survival?" I ask, putting the question to everyone. "Family!" they call out, almost together. "Right," Laura adds, "you need a strong family in order to believe you can do it . . ."

"Despite all odds," Enid finishes Laura's sentence. "And I'll tell you what else you need. Help from all kinds of people. You can't grow up as I did, thinking you can only depend on black people. Because, in the first place, it isn't true. Second, you're going to have to live in the world with all kinds of people."

I ask Enid how the black culture enters the desegregated classroom and she is adamant in her response. "When I'm in the classroom, I don't see color. I teach a lot of what might be called black history even though I'm the only black teacher in my school right now and only 20 percent of the children are black. I am teaching *history* to *children* and it is not a case of black or white. I try to teach the things I've learned. I didn't realize until I got to college that our country could do anything wrong. I'm not just referring to black experiences, but to the internment of Japanese Americans, the treatment of Chinese immigrants long ago, the lives of Native Americans, even here in North Carolina . . ."

"*Especially* in North Carolina," Louise and Laura chime in, smiling at each other. Louise looks around the table at all of us as if she is deciding whether or not to make a statement. "Look, it didn't matter if you were black or white, your education left out more than it put in. The thing I'm trying to do now is find out more about blacks and their contributions to the world. If I were white I'd want to be doing the same thing even if I didn't have a single black child in my class. It's not Afrocentric, it's history. And," she stops for emphasis, "*and* it has to be in the regular curriculum. We are one people, one nation, made of many different people. We must learn this together from the earliest age."

"Amen!" Enid and Laura call out.

"Funny thing," I say. "When the three of you began recounting your experiences during desegregation, I thought you might end up saying it wasn't worth the struggle. You're not saying that at all."

"No, we're not," Louise agrees. "We've talked about this before with lots of people at these conferences. I haven't met anyone who thinks we should go back to the way we were. If you're in an all-white or all-black school, there might be nothing you can do about it, but it shouldn't be the goal. At least you can integrate the curriculum."

"Tell Vivian about your school integration, Louise," says Laura. "She'll want to know about that."

"Okay. Now, my city has been court ordered to balance our schools at 60 percent white and 40 percent black. But next year we'll even go a step further. We've decided to put the 'special ed' children into the regular classes and, since there is usually a larger percentage of black kids in these classes, this will have the effect of further desegregating our schools. It's going to be voluntary at first, but more than half the teachers have agreed to do this, and as many whites as blacks. I'm real pleased."

We stack our trays and walk along together to the afternoon session, talking about the Blue Ridge Mountains in the distance. But my mind is on the stories I have just heard. These women, who grew up in a more segregated environment than most Northerners could imagine, are certain we must have integrated schools if we are to become "one people, one nation," as Louise insists. And yet, I remind myself, the sociology professor also grew up in a southern segregated school system, and he feels that black children do better in black schools.

"Louise," I whisper, as we take our seats in the darkened

auditorium, "couldn't there be some advantages for a black child in a black school?"

"You're asking the wrong question," she replies quickly. "When I taught in a black school, the brightest kids were favored over the slower ones. Furthermore, I myself was favored when I taught the so-called gifted children and was ignored when I was the special ed teacher. Okay. Then I moved to a white school and the same thing happened. The smart kids and their teachers got everything they needed and the others didn't. Now I'm in an integrated school and we're dealing out the same cards. This is not a racial thing. We have to change our snobbish feelings about early school success. *This* is what pits children against each other. You talk to any special ed teacher and you'll hear the same."

As I walk to Lorraine's room, a variety of Kwanzaa scenarios flash through my mind. He could have been on his way to Africa by now but I keep extending his stay in the Kingdom of Tall Pines. There's the unhappy Beatrix, who may need him to lift her out of a jealous mood, and after that, I may want him to come to the aid of the hapless pirates, once again under lock and key and no longer permitted to play with the queen's chess set. Perhaps, if Kwanzaa can convince them to give up their wicked ways, they might become his crew when his ship is ready to sail.

The fact is, I don't want to lose Kwanzaa just yet. He and Annabella and Prince Kareem give me another voice in the classroom that connects me to matters of black identity. Besides, I have not come to terms with my ignorance of his holiday namesake.

Lorraine is straightening up her desk when I come in. "I've been wanting to ask you something, Lorraine," I say even before I sit down. "How come in those early days you never told me about Kwanzaa? Sonya said, when I asked her, that it sounded 'too black.'"

"Too black? Yes, probably she's right," Lorraine replies, coming to the table where we have our conversations. "In those days, everything was either black or white to me. I remember you once asked me who were the people who lived in my neighborhood before it became black and I told you they were white people. This, of course, didn't answer your question. But I was unable to tell you what kind of whites because I didn't think in those terms. As it happens, they were Irish Catholics, but to me the world was black or white."

"You've changed in the past fifteen years," I comment. "So have I."

"The times they are a-changing. People want to talk about themselves now. Ten years ago those North Carolina teachers wouldn't have had such an open discussion with you. Even the history books are changing. Some day we'll no longer need a Black History month," she says, pointing to the pictures on her walls. "John Hope Franklin considers it another form of segregation."

Her mention of this respected black scholar brings a new question to mind. "What would he say to people who want black schools? Would he feel they are going backward, giving up the good fight?"

Lorraine answers by referring to another black scholar. "Derrick Bell says that racism is here to stay. We're spending too much energy fighting it. Just go about the business of living. Sure, we need affirmative action and equal opportunity programs, but racism itself isn't going to change too much. Those who want to return to black schools are saying, 'Let's put that energy into our own kids, into our black schools. Let's figure things out for ourselves and be the best of whatever we can be. Who cares if it's all black? As long as this school has everything any other school has, why worry about trying to change the way white people are going to be?'"

"But Lorraine, that can't be the meaning of all this struggle!" The words escape me before I can tone them down. "The classroom is the first place where racism can be fought. And most teachers *want* to fight it. They are not giving up. Now you've said this yourself: people are really trying to listen and learn how to tell everyone's story including their own."

Lorraine will not be distracted by my sermons. "Here is something you need to know, Vivian. For so long there has been this sense that anything black couldn't be good. We bought the whole feeling the world told us: you're no good."

"But your childhood was not like that," I say.

"My home was a safe haven," she replies, "but it was always hard for my parents. They would have liked better housing, better jobs. They made us feel safe, but they knew what I found out later after I saw the rest of the world, that anything all black was not considered good. Now we are saying: we can have something all black that can really be good."

"And the integrated school?"

"For most children," she says, "maybe an integrated school is fine. But, in order for some to operate from a base of strength, they've got to come out of a nurturing black school environment that is not in conflict with their homes. Then they can deal with the racism out there. And no two ways about it, the racism is going to be out there."

There is no ambivalence in Lorraine's words. Her vision of a "nurturing black school environment" rises forcefully out of her own experience. I continue to think about this conversation on my way to a conference in Alaska a day later and find myself repeating it to Lily, a Tlingit woman. She is both teacher and cook in a Tlingit Head Start center and has just given a workshop in story and song, sharing her native foods.

"I hear you," she says when I quote Lorraine to her. "Tlingit children would be better off if they could remain in native schools until they are much older. We have lived here for thousands of years but we are in danger of losing our language and culture. My granddaughter says to me, 'I am hungry for my own food, Mama.' She calls me Mama. 'I want some black seaweed, I want some red seaweed, I want a cracker with hooligan grease and I want berries for dessert.' She is not afraid to take this food to school for her lunch, as I would have been and as her mother would have been."

I try to imagine how such a lunch might look. Asian children in my class who begin school carrying native foods in their lunchboxes soon learn to ask for peanut butter and jelly sandwiches, to their parents' dismay. For Lily, too, food is an essential transmitter of culture.

"When I was little," she continues, "I went to an all-Indian school, a little green house down in the village, a happy place for me. Then, in the fourth grade, I made a big transition into public school. That was very hard. Most of the teachers were terrible to me. I was the child off in the corner. I didn't speak and no one spoke to me. Finally, in the seventh grade, I had a teacher who treated me like a human being. But in all of my years of school the non-natives never played with me or invited me to their birthday parties."

She does not call the others "white." By the end of our conversation I find myself doing the same, referring to everyone who is not Tlingit as non-native.

"How did you survive?"

"My mother was there for me. She taught me everything I know. She spoke Tlingit to me and kept it alive. She taught me the native food gathering and respect for food. I was at her side. I am a great believer in the parent as teacher. I wish we could go back to having an all-native kindergarten and primary grades. We have Head Start for native children but I wish it could continue."

"Until what age?"

"All the way through. There are schools that have all-native people and studies. I think that's good. There is so much to learn. When I was young we were not allowed to speak Tlingit in school. In some schools you were punished for speaking a native language."

"Lily, you feel as many African Americans do. But others say, we want our children to join the mainstream and have the same education as others. They worry about black children feeling like outsiders. How do you answer that?"

Lily looks away, and I wonder if I have offended her. "This is a hard question," she replies finally, turning to me. "Like they say, it's a white man's world. Our children will have to get out into that world. But my thinking is, if there were a lot of native children, from the beginning and through the grades, it seems as if the children would build up more self-esteem. They could hang on to their culture. Then, as they got older, maybe they could choose if they wanted to go to, as you call it, an integrated life. They could make the transition slowly."

"Could a non-native teacher learn to teach your children what they need to know?" I ask. "With your help, I mean."

Lily answers without hesitation. "For my grandchildren, I would always want to choose the native teacher. She is aware of the culture, aware of the food. This is important."

It is Lorraine herself who brings in my next visitors, a few days after I return from Alaska. They are a group of teachers from Ohio, observing in our school this week. "Here are some new opinions for you, Vivian, from the Buckeye State," she laughs. "I've been telling them about our discussions and they want to put in their two cents. They teach in black schools, so that should be interesting for you."

The three teachers she introduces to me do seem eager to describe their feelings and experiences. I have yet to come upon any teachers who were not ready and willing to discuss their circumstances, tell you what they know, and push the boundaries to discover more about the children they teach. The notion that teachers are not reflective or introspective is far off the mark. Of all the people involved in educating our children, the classroom teacher is most likely to be responsive to the intimate details of the changing environment.

Sue Ann is first to appear; the others will set aside time the following day. She comes from a rural New York white Catholic school background, kindergarten through college, and has been teaching for ten years in an inner-city black school in Ohio. I ask if she has ever felt the children in her class would benefit from having a black teacher who might know more of the context of their family and community culture.

"I do think about it," she tells me, "but only because it's being pounded at me lately, through the media, the school system, and especially from black people. 'What are you *not* doing for my child because you are white?' Sure, there's a lot about black culture I don't know, but this would be so if the children were Vietnamese or Polish or Jewish. I may not know a lot but I learn quickly. I go to the source, to older children, to black adults, and they fill me in. What's that language about, what's the meaning of this or that? I find it useful. People have to explain themselves and I have to explain myself. That wouldn't happen so much if we were all black, would it? Do I think a black teacher could serve them better? No, I don't. I have created a child-centered, hands-on curriculum that keeps evolving according to each child's needs. I think this approach serves all children well, no matter what their race."

The sun has suddenly broken through the gray overcast sky and we decide to continue our conversation on a park bench across from the school. "Can you give me an example of a piece of behavior or language that has caused you to get help in interpretation?"

"Rap music," Sue Ann says promptly. "There's a good example. I had a lot of trouble with that. But these rap singers are held up as heroes, so I went to people to find out more about rap. I was so against it at first I wouldn't use any song with a rap beat because I connected it to all the violent lyrics of the street. But after studying the subject, talking to black people, reading up on it in the library, I came to see it as a positive, vital expression for inner-city children. Now I look for rap songs with good lyrics. There are loads of them, you know. Even our drug resistance program includes rap songs. I still have my own favorite songs, of course, mostly American folk songs of the Pete Seeger variety, Burl Ives, and such, but we have rap too. The children like both."

"This is something I ought to do too," I say. "I'll talk to some high school students about rap. I've been avoiding the subject."

Sue Ann laughs. "You can't avoid it with *my* second graders. And there are other things I can't avoid. For example, this expression: 'I gotta use it.' The kids won't say anything else when they have to go to the bathroom. It bothered me. I tried every way I could to get them to use ordinary expressions. I'd rather hear 'I gotta pee.' Well, I gave up. This is what they say at home and in school. It was a battle I decided not to continue. Behavior is more important than whether they say, 'I gotta use it.'"

"What sort of behavior changes are you after?" I ask.

"The same as would exist in any class, white or black. I want children to listen to each other more patiently and respond carefully. I want us to be able to play nicely and have good discussions about issues that affect us."

"Are more of these discussions lately in the area of black culture and history?" I ask.

"Oh, absolutely. I make sure. I've got books that reflect black children, more than I used to. This is everyone's expectation, society's, the curriculum's, the system's. I pay more attention to black heroes when I'm researching a topic. We've just finished a unit on the Underground Railroad and I'm preparing for one on African folktales. I'll contrast a character called Anansi with our own Br'er Rabbit."

I tell Sue Ann about the Kwanzaa party and Mrs. Johnston's Anansi story. "Yes," she says, "for Kwanzaa I also called a parent. Frankly, I hadn't really understood it before last year. I wish I had a black teacher for a resource person, someone like Lorraine, whom I felt comfortable with, to come in and explain things to me. There are some things I'm vague about. I mean I can understand the issue of slavery and how that has carried into society today, but if I team-taught, let's say, with a black teacher, I'd learn more about the little details of life. Even so, I don't feel I'm insensitive to these issues or can't do a good job."

Sue Ann mentioned on our way outside that she had three white children in her class, and I ask her now if she has any concerns about them. "Oh, yes, I do," she answers. "I don't think we pay enough attention to the small number of white kids in our school. We keep talking about wanting the black children to succeed but what about the white children? Do they feel they are part of the community?"

"That seems a good point, Sue Ann. What do you think is

the best thing you do to produce this sense of community in your classroom?"

There is an eagerness in Sue Ann's reply that reminds me of the Canadian teachers. Schoolteachers are more aware than ever of this need to establish a real community in their classrooms. Perhaps it is because we are increasingly concerned about the sense of fragmentation in children's lives as well as in our own.

"One of the things I struggled to do as a teacher," she says, "was to learn how to let children know that emotions are okay, that it's all right to get angry, to be scared, to cry, to be upset. When you give out orders and don't bother to ask children how they feel about them, you destroy community. Community means you can be yourself, do what you need to do, talk about what's on your mind, no matter how long it takes you to state your case. See, I don't care how much of an Afrocentric or any other ethnocentric curriculum you have, there won't be a feeling of community unless this other curriculum I'm talking about comes first."

The second of the Ohio teachers stops by the next day after school and his wife joins him within the hour. John and Connie are black. He is a fifth-grade teacher at Sue Ann's school and she is the director of a Head Start school nearby. When I ask John if a white teacher can do as good a job as he can with black children he nods his head soberly. "Yes, if he or she conscientiously makes the effort to discover and include more of an Afrocentric curriculum. There needs to be an agenda that says outright—you, as a black child, come from this particular history with these heroes and these traditions. In other words, the white teacher should speak to the black children as *black* children besides being a part of the general population. White teachers can learn to represent the aspirations of black people along with the regular curriculum, so the black children realize *they* are included in what's being talked about, that they are not learning the history of someone else. Now I know this from first-hand experience. I did not understand that my family and I were part of what my teachers called the American heritage."

"Sue Ann worries," I point out, "that the white children in your school might feel that way, left out."

"I agree," John replies quickly. "In our school we have a small minority of white kids. You are either black or white, and we do tend to lump the whites together in a faceless group. That was done to me. 'The black boys this and the black boys that.' I watch myself. There are three white kids in my class this year: one is Croatian, one Italian, and one from North Carolina. I try to bring their cultures into the classroom community."

My final question to John, before his wife comes in, as it has been to all the teachers, has to do with the sense of community and how it is achieved. He answers, "I apply some of the Kwanzaa principles to our classroom. First, we help each other fulfill group goals. Second, we work hard to be our best. Third, maybe most important, we want our classmates to express themselves as individuals, to tell us or show us who they are, what they think and what they like to do. In other words, how they differ from everyone else."

"Is this harder to do when nearly everyone is black?" I ask. "Do you tend to take more for granted?"

"I think that's possible," he responds. "You know, we have a sign in our room too. Yours says, 'You can't say you can't play.' Ours says, 'Listen to me, I've got something important to say.'"

Connie walks in just as John finishes quoting his sign. She bursts out laughing. "This man is a great signmaker. My favorite was, 'You want me to listen to your idea? Then listen to mine!'" She plops down on a chair, obviously tired from a day of visiting our preschool classrooms. Turning to me, she laughs again. "It's been a long while since I've spent time with so many white children," she says. "We have only five in our entire school."

"What if you had a choice?" I ask her. "What if you could send your Head Start children on to an integrated school, all races and backgrounds, instead of the mostly black public schools they'll be going to? Which would you prefer?"

Connie smiles at her husband as if they have talked about this before. "That doesn't really matter to me," she replies. "As long as the learning environment is where it needs to be, it doesn't matter what the race or background of the children might be. The balance is not important to me. I fully appreciate integration for children and I like the idea, but if the environment is set up so that the children are learning, I wouldn't keep my children out of a black school. You can learn about all different kinds of people even if you have one race in a classroom."

"How would a class of all white children or all black children learn about each other?" I ask.

"It can be done. I've *seen* it done," Connie insists. "Through reading, field trips, adopting another school, exchanging ideas, but mainly through the *attitude* of the teachers. Busing children is a problem for me. Why travel an hour or more to go to a white school when there's a school nearby? Now at least we have open enrollment. You can go wherever you want if there are openings. I like that."

"By the way, where did you two send your own children?"

"To a neighborhood school," John replies. "They could have gone to a magnet school, probably the best in the city, but we thought we'd be more comfortable as a family in the local school. I'll tell you something. I'm the youngest of four and we went to white schools. Now we all send our kids to black schools."

Connie nods. "It's the same in my family," she says. "My sister teaches in Houston and she struggled with the same choice. There's a really good public school her kids certainly could have gotten into, but she did not even apply because it has so few black children. Good as it is, that school is having difficulty attracting black students. It's a shame when you think about it. They're trying to create a high-quality integrated school down there, but the times don't seem right for it."

I ask Connie about her own early school experiences, and she tells me that, like John, she went to white schools. "I did well. I felt more comfortable in a white school than John did. For me, it's always been a question of what the style of teaching is, the entire learning environment. As a Head Start director, what's important to me is play and respect for individual development. Children need to learn about their own culture, sure, and this seems to be what everyone is focusing on now. But I say we need to learn about all cultures, black, white, Asian, Hispanic, everyone's. As long as we meet the developmental and learning needs of children they'll be happy. Color doesn't matter to children."

"Nonetheless," I say, "some folks think black teachers will understand black children better."

"Not necessarily," she responds. "We've had black middle-class teachers who were not familiar with inner-city families and white teachers who were. Some people of any color simply have a better instinct for children. The trouble is, black and white teachers don't help each other nearly enough to understand their different cultures."

"Tell Vivian about the summer program you've helped organize," John urges.

"It's a six-week session," Connie explains. "We have teachers from pre-kindergarten all the way through third grade communicating with each other about all these issues, teaching styles, backgrounds, and curriculum preferences. We have more respect for each other now. We're trying to set up a common set of beliefs about how children learn and how teachers teach. And we've also been talking a lot about parent involvement. Most parents feel outside the loop. We need to accept their contributions more and create more open, friendly schools for the community. Without that you can't have a real community in the classroom."

It is difficult to dispute Connie's belief that most people are treated as outsiders in their children's schools. For the black parent in a white school or a white parent in a black school—or any other minority in either school—this must be an even more disturbing reality.

The question would seem to rest upon definitions of "insiderness." Connie welcomes parental "contributions," but the black parents in my class are even more specific. The Johnstons will "seek out teachers at every grade who are able to promote the good spirit of every child." Mr. Arnold says he'll watch carefully to make sure his children are not "put down," then tells a story of the ultimate put-down, the exclusion of black children from a community amusement park. Dr. Rudolph thinks our school would benefit from the "guidance" of black parents to better understand the needs of black children. All three families, it seems to me, are delicately positioned in a sort of limbo between waiting to be asked and watching for trouble signs. They tread lightly and hope for the best.

Oddly enough, of all the teachers I've spoken to thus far it is Sue Ann, from the most restricted of white backgrounds, who actively promotes contributions: she gets information and guidance from black parents and older students. She does it on her own and she does it because "community means you can be yourself." Sue Ann is determined to discover what the "yourself" is for the black children she teaches. Significantly, she is more comfortable asking black parents and older siblings for help than going to her own black colleagues, nor do they apparently go to her for information about the minority of white children in the school.

The idea that teachers from different cultures might become each other's resource people is simple to envision but apparently not easy to put into practice. It took me, after all, fifteen years to come to Lorraine. However, now that the connection has been made, the subject of black and white appears endless.

"How many teachers come knocking at your door?" I ask Lorraine. "You've mentioned a few."

"Well, just last week Barbara asked me about a boy in her class who claims she's picking on him because he's black. Unfortunately, he gets into lots of trouble with the other kids so this sort of response is a frequent occurrence. Barbara feels awkward about bringing up the matter of race with his parents, especially since he's the only black boy in the class."

"What did you tell her?"

"That first of all she shouldn't hesitate to discuss this with Carl's parents. However, before she does, she can use the problem as a learning opportunity for the boy and his classmates. I'd say, 'Carl thinks he's being picked on because he's black. So let's talk about exactly what he's being criticized for doing and see if it has something to do with being black.' Then call his parents, give them the full story, and ask for their advice."

This approach makes good sense to me, and you don't have to be black to make it work. "What if a white child in your class," I ask, "says something that sounds racist? Would you react in the same way?"

Lorraine ponders this for a moment. "I remember a discussion I was having with the kids, talking about the whole issue of slavery and all that came after. A white boy said to his black friend, 'Well, if it hadn't been for slavery you black people would not have been here anyway.' He seemed to be saying, 'We did you a favor by making you slaves and bringing you to this country.'"

"Couldn't his comment stem from inexperience or a poorly thought-out notion? Not from racism?"

"Oh, sure, though I did think he should have known better.

Anyway, I told him that what he just said could hurt a black person's feelings. But, maybe, I said, he meant to say something else. Could someone in the class help him to express himself differently? The children took the subject seriously. We had a good discussion. Everyone could see there are things you might say to a person to make him feel he is not equal to you. Finally, the black friend himself gave the white boy the right words. He told him, 'You could say to me that you're glad I'm your friend but you're sorry black people had to be slaves long ago.'"

I am curious to know how Mr. Arnold would have handled both incidents. That evening I call him and pose these "hypo-thetical" problems. Interestingly, he is as sympathetic to the child who seems to be justifying slavery as to the boy who cries "black."

"These kids are trying to figure out how the world works," Mr. Arnold says. "The first one may really wonder if the reason he gets into so much trouble is because he's black. He certainly hears plenty at home about all the troubles black folks have. I'd treat it the same way as if he'd said he gets blamed because he's left-handed. I'd ask the class to discuss it openly: what are the behaviors he's getting blamed for and are they connected to his racial identity? Now, the white boy also may have mismatched some logical connections. Listen, as a math teacher, I could tell you of amazing errors in logic from high school students! Any-way, this kid may be thinking of the old 'every cloud has a silver lining' cliché or, maybe, in his clumsy way, he's trying to explain that he's glad his black friend is here in this white class. Who knows? The point would be to let everyone help him find a better way to say how he feels."

"You seem rather nonchalant about this," I say. "These incidents actually took place."

He chuckles. "So I figured. There's enough real things happening to make it unnecessary to invent problems."

Although for me the perils and possibilities inherent in the integrated classroom seem most fully revealed in a black and white drama, an appreciation of any one diversity ought to set the stage for all the others. Yet I marvel at how few of these possible differences have entered my consciousness.

Having traveled east during spring break, I am ushered into the director's office of a small private school near Boston for a discussion about diversity. At first glance I feel disappointed. I did not expect everyone would be white.

Now, as the five women in the room introduce themselves, I am again reminded that to presume homogeneity in one race is as unfortunate an error as is the assumption of separateness and dissimilarity between races. There will be as many unexpected stories in this group as in any other I have encountered. My trainload of sensitivities and sensibilities is about to take on some new boxcars.

Linda and Marlene are each the parents of adopted Korean children; Eileen, a teacher in the school, has an adopted child who is part Puerto Rican and part black; Catherine is a lesbian mother; and Gloria, who teaches in the nursery school, came from Europe as an adult and lived with a black colleague and her family in a black community.

I speak first to Catherine because I am most curious about

her circumstances. "Do you consider yourself, as a lesbian parent, a minority?" I ask.

"Definitely, yes," she replies. "My daughter has two mothers and so her perspective on family life is different. The problem is not unrelated to those of racially mixed families, but there will be more discrimination against our child."

"Some people disapprove of racially mixed families," Eileen points out.

"I know," Catherine nods, "but there will be people, even in this community, who will not want their kids to come to our house. It hasn't happened yet because our child is young, and it is less likely to occur in this school. But it will happen."

She smiles at the director, Seymour, who has just walked in. "My partner and I have discussed all of this with Seymour. He makes us feel that our family can talk about themselves openly."

"Which her daughter already does easily," Gloria informs us. "I've heard Susie say, 'My mommies love each other,' and Lara, who also has lesbian parents, says her mommies are getting her a kitty. Everyone wants to tell us something: Mommy and Daddy took me to the zoo; we're going to have a baby; Grandma is living with us; Daddy has a new apartment; and so forth. Nothing is too unusual to talk about."

Turning to Marlene, Gloria adds, "Your Alice told us that she is Korean and you are not. The children are no more surprised at that than to find out Susie and Lara have two mothers each."

"Yes, our girl knows where she comes from," Marlene states. "When we heard on the news that a Korean ferryboat sank, she asked if her Korean mother was on that boat. We talked about it and she seemed reassured. Actually, the issue now is that she sees no one in the class who looks like her. Alice is only four but she has mentioned this several times. I told her there *are* other Asians in the school . . ."

"Twelve," Seymour says, "of whom four are in adoptive families."

"Okay, but so far," Marlene continues, "Alice is the only nonwhite in her family and the only Asian in her class. However, we do have many Asian friends and we know other adopted Asian kids of white parents."

But in school, at least, four-year-old Alice feels the absence of those who look like her. How important is this? Vijay's face flashes through my mind, then the faces of Rehei, Mashi, Jiroj, Cheng, all from past years—did I ever wonder if they were looking for Asian faces?

"Alice doesn't talk of it often," Marlene adds, "but it's interesting that even before she could speak, whenever she saw an Asian face, in a magazine or on TV or in the supermarket, she would point and smile. Only at Asian faces, mind you."

"This has also happened to us!" Linda exclaims. "We have two Korean children. The younger would call every Asian he saw 'Margaret,' his sister's name. And Margaret, who is older, also identifies more quickly with Asian children and is especially careful of their feelings. There's a Japanese boy in her class, a shy boy, and she is so eager to help him. At home she'll tell us, 'I asked Yoshi into our group today.'"

This conversation continues to have its déjà vu effect on me. I think of the second graders who visit us regularly. The older children come in to read to the younger ones. Normally their teacher and I pair the children in advance, but last year we let them come together spontaneously. As if guided by an unseen hand, her two Asian boys went directly to my Asian boys, though they were all from different countries, and my black girls sat beside her black girls.

Afterward, when I described the event to several black parents, they all took it as evidence that more black children are needed in every classroom. The one Asian parent I spoke to seemed unconcerned. "Our children live at home with many from our country," he said. "We are not worried that our son has only one other Asian child in his class." Unfortunately, I did not bring up the matter with any other Asian parents.

In the case of the black children I was more persistent. Soon after my conversations with the black parents, I invited several older black children, third graders, to come in and play. These were former students whom I knew still felt comfortable with me. But why had I created this opportunity for black children and not for the even fewer Asian children in the class?

Certainly the black parents' response was crucial to my decision but, in addition, I think the sociology professor was still on my mind. I wanted to tell him that the book is not closed as far as the integrated classroom is concerned. Only a few chapters have been written and there is much that can be done to improve the script. Or at least I needed to tell this to myself.

An interesting aspect of these playtimes with the third graders has been the increased use of "home talk," as Mr. Arnold calls it. The visitors, of course, play with everyone; they are very much in demand all over the room. But when they are involved with the black children we hear the familiar "Hey, girl, what you doin'?" "What's happenin', bro?" It is Lorraine's "kinship," plain and simple.

Now, as I listen to Linda and Marlene speak of their Korean children, I think again of Vijay. Bringing Kavitha into a Magpie story is not enough, nor even is his father's gentle tale of children playing in a stream near Calcutta. We need real Indian children playing in our classroom. Such arrangements can also be made for the Japanese, Chinese, and Hispanic children who arrive in equally small numbers. Perhaps their parents need more encouragement in order to express feelings about matters of isolation in the school community. And what of gay and lesbian families? I have never heard the subject mentioned until this conversation in Massachusetts.

Eileen's voice brings me back to the discussion. "Our little girl," she is saying, "being Puerto Rican as well as black, has so many aspects to her background that we placed her in a public school. Here there would be no one who looks like her. But when I brought her to the public school in my neighborhood, on the very first day someone in the playground called out, 'Oh, Juanita, there is your sister coming!' I was so thrilled. I said to myself, yes, this is good, they have the *people* to make the curriculum. The mix of people."

Marlene nods. "For your child this works well. But in our public school there would be even fewer Asian children. For us this is a better place."

"And for us too," Catherine agrees. "The subject of lesbian parents would never come up in a local school. Our friends tell us this. So we're better off here, at least for now."

"These are all issues the school cares about," Seymour says. "If I tell you about our family-tree project you'll get an idea of the sort of concerns we're trying to deal with. Something we've always done in the fifth grade is to ask children to research their family history and draw individual family trees."

The women raise their eyebrows at each other: the subject of family trees obviously strikes a discordant note, which is probably why Seymour brings it up. "Let's say I'm an adopted eleven-year-old," he poses. "How do I respond to this assignment when my life begins at a certain point and not in the past? It is especially difficult for the African American child, adopted or not, whose family tree goes back to slavery. Immigration by choice and by oppression are two different things."

"That's true," Gloria says. "Most of our children talk about coming to the land of the free. The black child is excluded from that experience. I learned this when I lived with my black friends. They assured me that though I had just come to this country I was, in many respects, freer than they were."

Does everyone whose roots go back to slavery feel a sense of shame? I've heard children at my school say with pride that their great-great-great-grandparents were slaves, and one of our teachers displays an old iron lamp, a treasured family heirloom, carried to light the way by her great-great-grandmother, who was a slave. The teacher lights the lamp at our Martin Luther King, Jr., assembly while we sing "This little light of mine, I'm going to let it shine!" What is stronger, I wonder: the image of forceful capture or the sense of being a witness?

"Tell me more about the family-tree project," I suggest. "You seem to be saying it has outlived its usefulness."

"We feel it has," Eileen responds. "The idea of a lack of history is scary for some children. My daughter, for instance, will never know at least one biological parent. To me, the family-tree project is offensive. She could do *our* family tree but not one with her true history. It pulls her in two directions, though she may not be aware that it does."

"Times have changed," Gloria adds. "Years ago the adopted child simply followed the family tree of the adoptive parents. Now there are so many concerns. That's why we discontinued the activity. More of our families are nontraditional in some way."

What exactly is the meaning of nontraditional, I want to ask. When my mother immigrated to Chicago in 1909 speaking only Yiddish, the majority of families in her public school were non-English-speaking and steeped in their own traditions. Were the few English-speaking families and the teachers the only ones who were called "traditional"? In any case, it seems more difficult now than it was then to know which part of a *non*tradition to recognize and which to ignore.

Before I can word my question, Eileen has another point she is eager to make. "No matter how nontraditional our families may be, this school still represents, on the whole, people who are well off. Affluent. They live in nicer and bigger houses than mine. The class issue is important. It's another reason our child will go to a public school."

There are people in my school, I tell the group, who also worry that we are too privileged, but Gloria feels the comparison falls short. "Yours is a large school," she says, "so it's not so obvious. In a small community like ours, if you are of modest means you are constantly reminded of what you can't afford.

Your classmates say, do, wear, and bring in things that are out of your reach. It's hard to deal with in the curriculum. We can study cultures, teach languages, and so forth, but the children see what they see."

"And, believe me, we do study every culture represented by any child," Eileen confirms. "Parents will come in—Linda and Marlene have done demonstrations of Korean holidays several times—but it is not the same as going to school with the whole mix of people."

No one in the room disputes Eileen's argument. In this small, privileged educational community there exists a great amount of fair-mindedness and respect for individual differences alongside an appreciation of the realities of the outside world. To what extent does the struggle to give voice to every concern make up for the absence of a "whole mix of people"?

Perhaps the habit of recognizing and accommodating the unique attributes of each classmate, whatever they may be, can be applied at other times to all the people one is yet to meet. As we continue to search for ways to identify and support each other's differences, we may discover that individuality is and always has been the greatest commonality we share. And some day, when nonconformity itself becomes the tradition, our children and we ourselves will be ready to accept as a matter of course the many images of humankind.

On to New Hampshire, where I meet Evelyn, who tells me she is an integrator. Surveying the white audience leaving the college auditorium after my talk I ask, "Whom do you integrate? Who are the minorities here?"

She smiles broadly. "Not the ones you have in mind. Our minority, if we called it that, would be children with learning problems or other handicaps. My job is to help them keep up with their classmates in a regular classroom. Sometimes I work with only one child, sometimes with several. This year, actually, I'm involved with a lot going on in the room."

"In Chicago," I can't help noting, "your title would be misunderstood. You'd be a learning consultant, or a resource person . . ."

"Or a special ed teacher? I'm all of those," Evelyn explains, "but my kids and I are just not kept separate any more. 'Inclusion,' we call it, and the teacher I'm with now really does include us as part of the classroom. Not all teachers will do that. But it works better if you do. These first graders watch out for my kids; they help them do things and bring them into activities."

"How does it work?" asks Rose, who has been standing with us outside the auditorium. She is a curriculum specialist in a school that serves a military base. "Is it like peer-tutoring? Do you plan for it or is it spontaneous?"

"Both ways," Evelyn replies. "Or, I should say, planned at first and now it happens because a lot of children see it as their responsibility. Let's say someone is unable to process verbal directions given to the whole class, a common problem. Another kid will take his hand and say, 'Mrs. Gilliam wants us to line up,' or maybe he'll sit with him and explain a game that was just put on the board or point to a line they're supposed to be copying. My kids need lots of repetition and support, so you're always welcome to come help or just be a pal and play."

"What a nice community feeling this must produce," I say,

imagining a chapter in which Kwanzaa teaches someone to read. Who could he befriend in this way? Beatrix the witch? Maybe she feels so left out of things because she's never been to school with the others. What if . . .? I snap myself back to the conversation. Evelyn is further explaining the effect of her system of cooperative learning.

"After a while, you see, my kids seem like everyone else because we apply what we learn about Timmy, let's say, to the so-called ordinary children. Turns out, of course, that everyone has some kind of hang-up. One of Timmy's problems is he gets stuck in a pattern of repeating a single phrase. Or he'll suddenly scream and run around. He's in a rut. So we talk about these things as a group and try to figure out how to help him. Then we realize that lots of people are in their own kind of rut: aggressive behavior, inappropriate language, bossiness, shyness, poor table manners, the usual. We learn to discuss each other's weaknesses and strengths in a helpful manner. For this I give credit to the classroom teacher. She sets the tone."

I find all of this fascinating. It is what Louise, the black teacher from North Carolina, wants to see happening. Children are not pitted against each other because of the way they learn or behave. Evelyn and her colleague use the differences inherent in a particular minority, in this case children who need extra time to accomplish certain tasks, to build a strong community based upon individual styles and social responsibility. In so doing they have extended the classroom's boundaries and deepened its sensitivities.

Rose looks worried. "Okay," she responds finally. "I have no problem with weaknesses of that sort, behavioral, learning, whatever. Those are considered weaknesses by anyone. But how about when something is *not* a weakness, like race, and yet unintentionally might be treated as one. We do have a few minority children in my school, mostly because of the military base, and I make sure the curriculum is multicultural and anti-bias. Sometimes when a black family arrives, they're afraid something unpleasant might be said to their children. We tell them we won't allow any child to be treated unfairly. We have frequent discussions with all the children about how easy it is to hurt someone by what you say. There are multiracial pictures and themes on the walls and in our books—but frankly, we're playing it by ear. And the guidebooks don't help much either."

"But Rose," Evelyn urges, "don't we all need to be instructed on how to act? Most people don't know in advance."

"You mean grown-ups don't know," Rose corrects her. "The children have no problems. Look, I've spent my entire life around here and never had a black friend. If I'd gone to school with black children it would be easier for me to know how to make things better for a black child."

I ask Rose if she would consider involving the child's parents in her dilemma, asking them to come in and help in some way, but she seems doubtful. "Part of me is thinking, 'Oh, what a great idea!' And part of me is saying, 'No, that would single out the child.'"

Evelyn is shaking her head. "That child is already singled out. If the parents are willing to come in and share stories of their heritage or their particular point of view or experience, wouldn't that be wonderful?"

Rose is unsure. "It might offend them to think we're inviting them in just because they're black. I find it confusing. I don't know if I'm supposed to convey the idea that we're color-blind or should I be talking about color and inviting the parents to come in. The anti-bias curriculum has me going in both directions."

Suddenly Rose begins to laugh. "This is really funny! I think I *am* color-blind. I told you before that our staff is all white? Well, we do have a black teacher, a wonderful woman. I just never think of her as being black."

"Couldn't she be your resource person?" Evelyn asks. "How does she feel about inviting the black parents in?"

"I've never asked her," Rose says smiling. "But I will. She's the one for me to begin with. Why didn't I think of that?"

By now several others have joined us. It is to them I pose my last question: "Is there any group of children that tends to be discriminated against in school? You know, put down in some way?"

The women respond as if in one voice and then laugh uncomfortably. "The poor!" Doreen, a preschool teacher, is quick to explain. "You can see we've talked about this before. The teachers know who is poor and, very often, there are lower expectations for them. There's not the black and white issue here, so there's the issue of poor children."

Shelly and Gladys teach together in a second grade. "If you are poor," Shelly says, "teachers will just assume you are not exposed to reading, that you are less socialized, less cared for, not as bright. There is definitely prejudice concerning the poor."

"The thing is," Gladys concludes, "we tend to be so judgmental. Even people who claim to be anti-bias. It's easy enough to be unbiased about groups you don't have, but you'll find someone to be biased about, someone right there in your class. We all do. You have to listen to yourself carefully. I'm working on that. It's there all right. And you pass it on to the children. But at least we *are* talking about it somewhat."

While I am flying home it occurs to me that several old premises of mine need to be reexamined. Homogeneity, I have stated, is fine in a bottle of milk but not in a classroom. What is this quality I call homogeneity? Does it exist in any classroom or is it found in the perception of the beholder?

Are the children in Evelyn's room cut from the same cloth because they are of the same race? She, in fact, sees them as a mixture of different kinds of learners and behavers; her democratic community develops out of that premise. Janet Albright emphasizes the African American culture in her curriculum, but she once told me that her children are artists, storytellers, and inventors. Surely no one paints the same picture, tells the same story, or invents the same idea. Furthermore, in her unit on Freedom Fighters she includes Judah Maccabee and Pancho Villa, though there are no Jewish or Mexican children in the class.

This notion of homogeneity may well lie in the attitude of the teacher. Perhaps if we called ourselves *integrators* we would be better at identifying the "minorities" built into any group, those who act, feel, look, think, or learn differently. Then each child's special attributes could be included in the common culture.

Another point: it has seemed to me that in a multiracial

classroom we are more likely to recognize and accept these different attributes. Yet we always appear to be in the position of reacting to certain differences and ignoring or even condemning others. "You'll find someone to be biased about," Gladys warns us, and we are in sober agreement. It cannot be denied.

Mrs. Johnston and Mr. Arnold say the same thing, though they are certain that, in a white school, the black child may be the first target of bias. Doreen, teaching far away from the classrooms these black parents describe, intuitively understands their accusation. "There's not the black and white issue," she maintains, "so there's the issue of class."

This *habit* of bias is our common vulnerability. "We tend to be so judgmental," Gladys says, much as Lorraine insisted during an early conversation: Why do we have to be so judgmental? Lorraine, of course, was referring to the acceptability of a variety of classroom profiles, and Gladys is thinking about the individuals within a single room. In either case, it seems clear that, whether we teach in a white, black, or variably integrated environment, we probably dig ourselves into some kind of rut based upon a private collection of biases and limitations. Little Timmy's verbal rituals may yield more easily to peer analysis and mutual comparisons than do the unexamined attitudes of those of us in charge of the store.

Even so, wherever I go, from the tree-lined hilly streets of a quiet New England town to the housing developments of a Midwest inner-city neighborhood, from college town to factory town, big city or farmland, I can barely get my questions out before the teachers reveal their visions of an anti-bias, multicultural, child-centered, family-oriented, egalitarian *community-in-*

the-making. There is a new thrust of energetic idealism out there. It comes in many forms, and I feel it most when I am talking to schoolteachers.

Furthermore—and this is what fills me with hope—more and more teachers are accepting as a personal responsibility the day-to-day clearing away of the cobwebs of indifference. They attend endless conferences and study groups and read through piles of curricula and official memoranda, all of which offer solutions to a multitude of problems. But it is the teachers themselves who examine the lives of their own students and try to imagine a better world for them.

This is as it must be. In the final analysis, it will always be the classroom teacher who has the power to lift the spirit of the individual child and beat the drums for the communal dance. Ngoma, ngoma, ngoma . . .

The pilot's announcement of our descent into O'Hare hurries me, as it always does, into a concluding bit of rhetoric. Isn't Eileen's faith in the "whole mix of people" still the best hope for a democratic society? Don't we owe our schoolchildren as early a beginning as possible to this lifelong process of learning to work and play agreeably with a great variety of people?

Yes, to both questions, I scribble in my journal. But we can't wait for the outside world to deliver these nicely balanced classes. We must figure out, each in her own way, how to care for whatever group of children enters our classroom. We must teach them how to care about themselves and about each other. We must listen to their individual stories and try to imagine the stories that all the children *who don't look or sound like us* might tell if they were in our classroom.

Each in her own way. But which way, of all those I am hearing, makes the most sense? The truth is, I find myself understanding and agreeing with them all: each seems to hold a piece of a solution to an important problem. Every encounter now exposes a point of view that is immediately applicable in my own class- room. Tomorrow, I have already decided, I'll have a discussion with the children about the fate of the only Asian child in a non-Asian classroom.

Teacher:	Kavitha is the only person from India in her classroom. No one looks like her. I wonder how she feels about that.
Martha:	Vijay looks like her.
Teacher:	That's true, but Vijay is in *our* classroom. Who does Kavitha go to school with?
Jeremy:	Raymond. And Annabella. Does Beatrix go to that school? Or is she too old?
Teacher:	No, she's not too old, I'm sure, but so far she doesn't go.
Kesha:	Beatrix thinks witches aren't supposed to go to school. Alexandra is there, but anyway, no one can look like someone else unless they are twins.
Annie:	That boy in the library, that one who talks to Mrs. Paley, he looks like Vijay. Is he your brother?
Vijay:	I don't have a brother. That's Dilip.
Teacher:	Vijay, do you think Kavitha wishes there were another child from India in her classroom?

Vijay:	In her real or pretend classroom?
Teacher:	The one in my Magpie story.
Rasheem:	Where is her real classroom?
Jeremy:	That's the place where she really lives when she's not in the story.
Rasheem:	Oh, yeah, in that place there's plenty of people that look like her.
Teacher:	But in Schoolmistress's school, do you think she'd like to see someone who wears a sari, as she does?
Kesha:	Annabella could put on a sari. All of the girls could. Then Kavitha would think she's in India.
Martha:	Also, they could talk like her. She could tell them what the words sound like where she comes from.
Teacher:	That reminds me of Kesha's story about the girl who speaks Spanish. She was so happy when she found a place where everyone understood her. By the way, Kesha, do you enjoy having Jenny and Aila come to play?
Kesha:	Yes. Can Andrea come too?
Teacher:	Who is Andrea?
Kesha:	She's that white girl that always says hello to me. She's Jenny's friend. With the ponytail.
Teacher:	Sure, we could invite Andrea. We could invite Dilip, too. Would you like that, Vijay?
Vijay:	Yes.

Rasheem: Hey, that's good. Ask him could he bring that brother he was with.

Teacher: A black boy? What's his name?

Vijay: That's Peter. He's on my bus. He lets me sit with him sometimes.

Teacher: Okay, we'll send a note to Andrea, Dilip, and Peter. Hmm, this is interesting. One is white, one is Indian, and one is black.

Martha: Like in our classroom, right? Rasheem, is that boy Dilip's brother?

Rasheem: Naw, you just call someone a brother if they're black, that's all.

"So you see," I tell Lorraine after school, "the children don't want just one category of person invited in to play. By the way, Rasheem explained to Martha what a 'brother' is: 'You just call someone a brother if they're black, that's all.'"

Lorraine laughs. "Even kindergartners can inform each other about their own culture," she says. "They are most often their own best resource. But sometimes an adult needs to step in and help."

"Like the hair discussions? Or the one where the boy figured out the black kids wouldn't even be here if not for slavery."

"I've got another example for you," Lorraine says. "It just happened. Lorna and her fourth graders were talking about the black market. Part of a social studies unit. A boy asked, 'Why are so many bad things called black?' Lorna said she could see the black kids' hackles rising."

"It *is* sort of an insensitive question," I suggest. "I mean, shouldn't a fourth grader understand the effect his question would have on the black children?"

Lorraine sees the event in a positive way. "I think it was a sincere question. Here is a white boy who suddenly realizes that something is wrong with the way 'black' is used. Anyway, Lorna called me in to speak to her class."

"Good idea. A black teacher's ideas would have a greater impact."

"Perhaps. I started out by saying how powerful language is, how words can make you feel wonderful or terrible, strong or weak, ugly or pretty. 'Black' is one of those words that over the years has been very sensitive for black people. I told them that before 1960 it wasn't beautiful to be black. Our black hair was not beautiful, our black skin, our black noses, nothing about black was beautiful, not even among ourselves. Then we talked about expressions like black sheep, a black look, a black day, black magic, black-hearted, and so on. We made a list. They even looked in the dictionary and found blackmail, blacklist, blackguard . . ."

"Did they know all those words?" I ask.

"Some of them. They got the idea. Black cat was one they could hardly stop talking about. I told them that in the middle sixties and seventies we black people began to realize we had a lot to be proud of and that black was not ugly, it was beautiful. That's why I still use it, in addition to African American. Once it became beautiful I wanted it to stay beautiful. Okay, then I had the kids make a list of good things called black."

"Was it a shorter list?"

"At first, yes. But then, once they got started, it grew. They wanted black cat to be on the good list, maybe because they could all see that the notion of a black cat bringing bad luck was a silly superstition. They liked 'black hole' a lot, they thought it was a wonderful scientific term. And *Black Beauty* from the book they were reading, black-eyed Susan, blackboard, black belt, black gold, black-tie party, and so on."

"I suppose you discussed what substitutes could be used, a mean heart instead of black-hearted?"

"Oh yes, they loved doing that. It was a great lesson in adjectives, by the way. One girl said she didn't realize how damaging ordinary language could be and how important it is to be careful of what you say. I told her this was the whole point of our discussion. Sure, I wanted to talk about black and blackness. But more important, the issue is language and how you talk to people. A Jewish girl said she hated it when people used 'kinky' to mean weird behavior since her hair is kinky. Then a black girl laughed and said, 'So how do you think *I* feel?'"

"Were the black children as forthcoming as the white children?"

"Yes, except for one girl. But I knew her and I knew that blackness has been a big issue for her. She didn't say a word but you could tell she was soaking everything in, feeling good about the discussion, smiling even. It's a sensitive subject for her. She's very dark skinned and, because of certain aspects of her background, she's not yet ready to feel that black is beautiful. This discussion was good for her."

I stop by to see Lorraine the next day. There is a question on my mind that won't wait. "Lorraine, would the girl who worries about being black be happier in a black school?"

"I'm not sure," she replies. "This is a complicated story. Maybe she *would* feel better about herself in a black school. But her family is not from America. They don't identify too much with African Americans. As I said, it's complicated."

"You mean it's not black or white?" I jest. "Ugh! Let's get rid of that expression too, shall we? It's too divisive. Better say things are never just one way or the other. Which is true, by the way. Remember when you urged me not to be so judgmental? Well, I think I *am* becoming less so."

Lorraine gives me one of her dazzling smiles. "I've had the feeling you've been rethinking some things."

"It really pays to listen to a whole bunch of people," I say. "The other day I heard about a Wisconsin elementary school that teaches every aspect of its program in two languages, English and Spanish, on alternate days. One day everyone speaks English, and the English-speaking children, who are mostly black, do the tutoring. Then the next day Spanish is the language and the Spanish speakers are the helpers. Even a few years ago, I would have thought it sounds too gimmicky. Now my first reaction is, why not?"

"Why not, indeed?" Lorraine agrees. "It makes sense to me too."

"Say, I just realized something! It makes sense to the children. In the discussion I was just telling you about, my children were figuring out how a story-character named Kavitha, from India, could feel more comfortable in a classroom with no other Indian children. The solution was obvious to them. Kavitha would teach her language to everyone and all the girls would put on saris. Have you noticed how quick children are to copy someone else's mannerisms and expressions? They love taking on new roles. They *believe* in multiple identities."

Lorraine has been leafing through an educational journal. "There's a story in this issue, I think, about a school in California in which Spanish, English, and *Korean* take turns. I'm not sure how it's done, but again, why not?"

We seem to be playing a version of "Can You Top This?" "Okay, ready for this one, Lorraine? What about a classroom, a regular classroom that includes several deaf children, in which spoken English and *sign* language are used together for everything?"

Lorraine looks startled. "How does it work? Are the deaf children lipreaders too?"

"It's exciting to think about, right?" I am almost giggling. "This has got to be the ultimate metaphor for *inclusion.* The entire group has to learn a new language if full communication is to take place."

"So tell me," Lorraine demands, "where is this remarkable school? I'd like to visit."

"I'm sorry. It doesn't yet exist, as far as I know." Lorraine's expression dissolves. "I didn't mean to trick you," I apologize. "I just wanted to see if your reaction was the same as mine. I had a conversation with a speech professor from Texas who has spent years teaching and studying deaf children. In order to do this she has learned to sign fluently. She's very big on the idea of inclusion. What I have just described would be her dream classroom."

"Is it possible?" Lorraine wants to know.

"When I asked her that she said, 'Why not?'"

Even the birds stopped to listen when Kwanzaa sang. "Follow the drinking gourd! Follow the drinking gourd!" His voice carried this song of the Underground Railroad to every tree in the forest. As if in a dream, Kwanzaa saw the faces of all those who had helped him escape to freedom. "The old man is a'comin' to show us the way, follow the drinking . . . Wha? What's going on! Help!"

The ground beneath him was giving way and he felt himself falling. He had stumbled into that old trap Beatrix had once dug when she wanted to catch Annabella for her very own playmate. Poor jealous Beatrix.

Down, down, tumbled Kwanzaa, fortunately landing right-side-up on a pile of soft moss. "What kind of mischief is this?" he bellowed.

"No kind of mischief," Beatrix muttered. "If you had stayed on the path you wouldn't have fallen into my cave. You're Kwanzaa, aren't you?"

He stared at the raggedy-looking girl who stood glaring down at him. "And you must be Magpie's friend Beatrix."

"Friend? I think not!" She stamped her foot. "You're the friend! He's forgotten all about me."

Kwanzaa was surprised. "Didn't you receive his letter? I wrote it for him myself and he sent it by crow to your mother's house."

"Ha!" Beatrix laughed scornfully. "I left before it came. Anyway, Magpie knows I can't read." She paused a moment. "What did the letter say? Not that I care."

"It was about how much he misses you and how much your help is needed to build a new room for Schoolmistress." Kwanzaa stood up and smiled at Beatrix. "You know, I couldn't read either until about a year ago. Then a kind old man taught me to read. I can do the same for you. One favor always leads to another."

Beatrix stepped back in alarm. "I don't know. There are so many words." Then, shyly, she said, "But could you show me my name, please?"

Kwanzaa kneeled down and, with his finger, printed seven letters on the dusty floor of the cave. "'B-E-A-T-R-I-X!' There it is. Your first word."

The young witch's eyes opened wide. "Is that really me? How pretty it looks!" Slowly she repeated each letter as Kwanzaa took her finger and helped her copy them all. "B-E-A-T-R-I-X," she spelled over and over. "I can read and write my name!" she shouted, dancing round and round until she collapsed in a dizzy heap. Then up she sat. "Now show me how to write 'school,'" she demanded.

School? Ah, so this is why Beatrix feels so left out, thought Kwanzaa as he printed her new word. It's because she doesn't go to school with the others. "Speaking of school, Beatrix, I've often dreamed of going to a real school one day. How about you? Shall we march right over to Schoolmistress's house and ask if we can be her newest students?"

Beatrix grew quiet and glum. After a while she said, "School is not for me, Kwanzaa. I've seen those kids. They live in regular houses, they're cleaner than I am, and their clothing isn't torn. They won't like me."

"But Annabella, Alexandra, and Raymond like you. They don't care what you wear."

"That's because they know me. We've had adventures together. To the others I'm just a witch and they think all witches are bad."

Kwanzaa did not argue. He decided instead to pay a visit to Schoolmistress and ask for her advice.

"What did Schoolmistress tell Kwanzaa?" Kesha wonders. She and Martha have remained on the rug after my story.

"I haven't written that chapter yet," I say, showing them the empty pages. "What do you think her advice should be?"

Kesha wrinkles her brow. "Are there other witches in the forest?"

"Well, yes, I think there might be other witches."

"Then, *if* there are," Kesha declares, "let them have their own school. That way Beatrix will get used to school. After that, she can go to Schoolmistress's school."

Martha doubts if the plan will work. "See, she'll just want to stay in the witches' school 'cause she'll be used to it too much."

Kesha has another idea. "Then let her go to one school in the morning and one in the afternoon. And when she's older let her decide which one she likes better." Martha smiles approvingly.

It seems a sensible plan to me too. "How about if I have Kwanzaa and Schoolmistress say exactly what you two have just said. And then we'll see what happens." Kesha and Martha are as pleased as when they invent their own stories, but I am wondering why they have ignored the part of my story that seemed most important to me.

"Beatrix is worried that the children won't like her because she looks different and she doesn't live in a house."

"No, they don't mind," Kesha assures me. "They know some people are supposed to be different."

*S*ometimes Lorraine and I exchange books. She has given me Gloria Naylor's *Mama Day* and I've brought her Alex Kotlowitz's *There Are No Children Here*. Today we've decided to discuss them both.

"He didn't have the trust," Lorraine comments about a central character in the Naylor book. "He didn't trust Mama Day to take care of everything; he didn't trust time to do the healing."

"But nothing was ever explained to him," I argue. "The women resented having to explain their ways to a Northerner, to an educated urban black man. They didn't trust him but he was expected to trust them."

"Maybe that's Naylor's story," Lorraine says. "There's no compromise possible between these two worlds; rural southern black traditions can't be explained. The Old South is foreign to me too, you know. My grandmother came up from Mississippi seventy years ago. I'm second-generation Chicago."

"Are you any more familiar with the urban scenes Kotlowitz describes?" I ask.

She shakes her head. "No, I'm not. Those tragedies, that sadness and violence and despair. Just a few miles from where we sit."

"Lorraine, did you have the feeling I had that, in the end, the people who make the difference in that project are the school-teachers? They make a spelling bee as magical as Mama Day's incantations."

Lorraine sees my point and takes it further. "You dodge bullets on the way home from school, then you bury yourself away from the windows in case there's a stray bullet, and you repeat the letters of each spelling word over and over as if they will save you."

"What an incredible thing!" My excitement is palpable when such connections are made. "It reminded me of John Hersey's book *The Wall*, about the Warsaw ghetto. The Jews hid under the streets when the Nazis came. Hersey describes the way people crawled through the sewers, at the height of the violence, to get to a *poetry* reading. This is the great human factor, Lorraine. People can be killed by bullets and drugs but spelling bees and poetry readings will go on. To me, the heroes of the Kotlowitz book are the teachers and the schoolchildren."

As we repack our book bags, Lorraine tells me about a friend who teaches in one of the schools in a project. "Her principal said this to her: What our school has to be is a safe harbor. Whatever else is going on in these kids' lives, we can't control or change it. But when they cross our threshold, this is a safe harbor. We *teach* these children, and no one has a greater responsibility."

My mind reels at the thought of what this principal and her teachers must overcome. "Yet she expects her teachers to do what Kesha's mother demands of us, to promote the good spirit of every child. My lord, if it can be done where there is gunfire on the streets, then it can be done anywhere!"

"That's right," Lorraine replies. "In a safe harbor every child finds a ship that fits . . ."

"And is taught how to sail."

Where children's lives are imperiled on the way to school, the image of school as a safe harbor is vivid and uncompromising. It is difficult to adjust the perspective to fit my own classroom. To accomplish this, I must think back to my childhood and ask why my school never seemed a safe place. Over the years, I have come to know and to accept the answer: I could not be truthful about anything that worried me.

Now, as a teacher, I measure safety along this yardstick of fearless self-incrimination. I wait for the children who are not afraid to unburden themselves. Sometimes their problems seem disarmingly simple; at other times their anxieties pull me toward the mirror of my own unresolved fears.

"Some people they get real hungry," Michael says cautiously one day. "And they don't know when they're going to have lunch and they're afraid to ask the teacher."

I study Michael's face. He is as serious and concerned as I have ever known him to be. "Are you that person who gets hungry?" I suggest. "And am I the teacher you are afraid to ask?" He sits beside me and begins to draw his daily representation of erupting volcanoes. "You must think I'll be annoyed if you ask me," I continue, "but I wouldn't be. We'll eat after music, in about forty-five minutes. Take a cracker now if you like."

Michael is not relieved. "I'm afraid you'll say it's too long until we eat and then I'll be sad and I'll get into trouble and you'll send me to a dark . . . I mean you'll . . ." He recognizes a feeling of dread but can't imagine the likely outcome.

"Hey, what are you two talking about?" asks Jeremy, always curious about private conversations.

"May I tell him, Michael?" He nods. "Michael says that sometimes he gets real hungry and he's afraid to ask me when lunch is. And that makes him sad and he thinks he'll get into trouble."

Jeremy understands immediately. "Oh, yeah, that's just like me in music. I don't know if I'm going to be asked something that I don't know how to do it. I'm afraid of getting into trouble that way."

"And do you get into trouble?"

Jeremy takes a moment to consider my question. "No, just from running around and from not waiting."

"This is interesting," I tell the boys. "Here it is almost the end of May, and I've just found out something you're each afraid of that I didn't know before. Let's talk about this with the whole class after music. Someone might have an idea for us. Meanwhile," I say to Michael, opening the cracker tin, "take something to eat on the way to music."

When the group returns, Michael, Jeremy, and I describe our conversation, to which I add, "Two boys are having the same sort of problem with two different teachers. They're afraid of getting into trouble if they . . ."

"That's because they're embarrassed to do a wrong thing," Martha decides.

"Because then you're shy of the teacher," Edward explains, "from not sitting still and waiting."

"I'm not shy of the teachers," Annie states, "but I'm scared of if I'm going to make friends."

The children do not consider Annie's comment a non sequitur: the subject is fear. "Martha's your friend," Jeremy reminds her, but she shakes her head. "What if she likes someone better? Now she likes to play with Kesha."

"I'm your friend," Kesha responds quickly, prompting a general murmur of "me too."

"I hope Annie feels better now," I say, "but how about Michael and his lunch problem?"

Martha offers a solution. "Let him eat something small from his lunchbox whenever he's hungry. That reminds me, you were mad at me because I said there's no Santa Claus."

"Mad at you?" I am momentarily startled. "Oh, I remember that! Did I seem angry? I'm sorry. I only meant to say that when a Jewish family doesn't celebrate Christmas it's best for them not to say something that might spoil the holiday for others."

"You scared me."

Her words strike where I am most vulnerable. "I'm glad you're telling me this, Martha. It embarrassed you that I wouldn't let you tell us what your family believes. I'm sorry I did that."

"Hey, that's like me in music," Jeremy says. "I want to tell the teacher I don't believe in that activity because I won't know how to do it."

I gaze gratefully at the assemblage of truth-tellers on the rug before me. "This is an important conversation we are having. You've been talking about what embarrasses you. Very few people will do that. Even grown-ups are afraid to do that. I feel I am with brave people. When I was small I was not so brave. We'll discuss this more later, but all this excitement makes me hungry. Let's eat."

The chronology of these events is significant. Each child in turn has revealed a hidden anxiety, a source of embarrassment. One revelation has led to the next, culminating in an accusation by a Jewish child against the very one who should have understood her best, me, a Jewish teacher. In this instance, sharing the same culture did not produce a safe harbor. I had reacted, back in December, as if Martha's statements threatened me, in the way Mr. Arnold expects white teachers to behave toward black children who reveal their family's beliefs.

It is Kesha, finally, who uses fantasy to explain Martha's dilemma, something I had been unable to do. After lunch she dictates a story for us to act out.

> Once upon a time there was a princess who never celebrated Christmas. She had only celebrated Chanukah and she wondered what Christmas was like. And she asked her

mom if they could celebrate Christmas and she said yes. So that year they celebrated Christmas.

Do I find it easier to deal with black and white issues than with the position of a Jewish child in an integrated classroom? As I nervously contemplate this possibility, a memory sweeps over me, something I learned as a child in Hebrew school. "A person who shames a fellow being publicly," it is stated in the Pirkei Avot, the Sayings of the Fathers, "though he be learned in the Torah and perform good deeds, shall have no share in the world to come."

This must be the meaning of safe harbor for me: it is a place where you are able to tell the truth about yourself and not feel ashamed. Sometimes, of course, the teacher must help you search for these truths because you are not always able to explain who you are.

A Native American once told me that her children's school gave them no "safe passage." "What we teach at home is not respected or even known in school," she said. "Among our people, for example, it is considered improper to make oneself appear smarter than others. But the teachers, who are mostly white, mistake our children's reticence for dullness or rebelliousness. The children feel ashamed. This is wrong."

The idea of a "safe passage," which is to say a secure continuity between home and school, was not a subject for discussion when I was a child. The main point of school, as I perceived it, was to forget about home.

It is in comparison to the schools of my childhood that I

measure the changes I find today. The metamorphosis is remarkable. Not only has the curriculum exploded into a multitude of cultures but, more important, there is the realization, in theory if not always in practice, that the individual family has the right to see itself reflected in the school culture.

The contemporary concept of diversity that began with abstractions of race and ethnicity, then expanded to embrace the notion that children who learn or behave in different ways do not need to be segregated, now seems ready to allow families to come in and talk about themselves, their people, and their children's self-image.

"How can we possibly deal with all these issues?" bewail the teachers. "There is no room for even one more point of view!" Then along comes another story and the process begins anew. Once the classroom is opened to the stranger and homeborn alike, the door can never again be closed.

I do not imply that we already know these truths. However, we are on our way to this knowledge. Or are we? Is it merely talk, just another social studies unit? The sociology professor wants, for his child, a deeply felt experience in a school where learning and lore provide kinship not conflict, community not isolation.

Conflict cannot be avoided. A child is more than the sum of a particular culture, and we are limited in our ability to empathize with each other's passions. Moreover, feelings of isolation occur even in the most familiar community.

But, this notion of kinship: what a powerful image to ponder. More than anything else Lorraine has spoken of, her yearning for kinship in a school setting stirs my curiosity and emotions.

The kinship she finds in a black school has nothing to do with color, she says, and yet when she talks about "people of color," her voice changes and her face glows. I must return to this subject with Lorraine, especially since it emerges in the classroom from time to time and, almost always, it is the black children who bring it up.

"Are people from India as brown as me?" Kesha asks, studying Vijay's mother at the next table. Mrs. Shah has come to tell us a story and has stayed for lunch.

"Some are," I reply. "Vijay's mother is as brown as you are."

"You can't be Indian just from putting on a sari, you know. And the dot." She hands me her yogurt to open.

"Are you thinking about Kavitha?" I ask. "You had said the others could wear saris and pretend to be like her. Then she wouldn't feel so lonely."

Kesha shakes her head. "Uh-uh, they can't pretend that. Only Annabella can. And I can. Not if you're white you can't." She hesitates, struggling with her thought. "I mean you could *pretend* but you can't *be*. Don't you think Dilip is darker than me?"

"Maybe he is. By the way, have you noticed that Vijay smiles more whenever Dilip comes to play?"

"Vijay would rather to play with Peter," Kesha assures me. "Brown people—I mean brown *really* people—are nicer to play with. In my old school I could play with everyone."

Her face lights up at the thought of her nursery school. "I can still go there in the afternoon. They're so glad to see me. They hug and kiss me like crazy. I can't hardly breathe! We laugh so much. I say, 'Hey, girl, you killin' me!'"

We sit together, stirring our yogurts. Then I ask, "Kesha, could we make this school be more like your old school?"

My question surprises her. "No way! It can't be!" she replies. "But anyhow, this is my *real* school, you know." She cleans her place at the table and carries her lunchbox to her cubby. On the way she calls out to Martha and Annie in the doll corner. "Don't forget, I'm the teenage sister!"

Kesha seems so confident and happy playing with the white girls, I think as I finish my lunch. Will she read this book one day and say, "No, that's not the way it was at all. I felt dumb and ugly the whole time!"? Or will she remember Princess Annabella and know that this classroom tale could not have been told without a black girl named Kesha in the starring role.

At the potluck supper, a few days later, I sit down next to Mrs. Arnold, Jeremy's mother, and play with her baby for a few minutes. Then I ask if she is still thinking of sending Jeremy to a neighborhood school.

"We talk about it a lot," she says, smiling uncertainly. "It doesn't have to be the one in our neighborhood. In fact, I'm going to visit some other schools next week." She searches in her bag for a pacifier and continues. "Jeremy is having a good year. I know that. But I do have to wonder if this is the best place for us to be. As a family. My husband is more optimistic about this school than I am."

"You'd feel differently if we had more people of color," I suggest.

The directness of my response seems to help Mrs. Arnold relax. "Not just people of color. More African Americans, both children and teachers." She looks at me, wondering how far to go in her explanation. "Look, I know the teachers here mean well. But it's still *them* defining *us*. What if you Jewish people had been defined by others over the centuries, some of whom were anti-Semites? And this was part of your heritage. You are a strong people because you've always defined yourselves. We have to do the same."

Jeremy runs up and squeezes into the baby's space on his mother's lap. She helps him find a comfortable position while she completes her thought. "These are hard times for us, but we are a joyous, deeply religious people, devoted to family, church, and community. Leaders in every area of life have come out of these nurturing places. It's our way. We need to study ourselves to know that."

Mrs. Arnold's reference to the Jewish people startles me. She is not the least bit awkward talking to me of my people because she is securely connected to her people. "Defined by others." Are my Kwanzaa stories an attempt to define others? If so, then why, in the telling of them, do I feel a profound sense of kinship with the black children?

"Jeremy brings us a lot of information about African American heroes," I tell Mrs. Arnold. "Yesterday, he and Kesha answered a question about Malcolm X. Someone wanted to know why a boy in the library had an 'X' on his shirt."

"What did you say, son?" Mrs. Arnold asks.

Jeremy hops off his mother's lap. "I said it's an African name.

Because he was giving speeches in church to be more free everyone and to know about Africa." Jeremy sees his mother is pleased. "Sorry, Mom, I gotta leave now. Those guys are waiting for me," he says, pointing to the block corner.

Mr. Arnold comes to take his turn holding the baby. I want to ask him if my Kwanzaa stories help create a bond between the black children and me but it seems too self-serving. Anyway, sitting here with Jeremy's family I can answer my own question, in part. The fact that I enjoy being with them, talking to them, finding out what they think and—I have to admit—hearing Mrs. Arnold refer to the Jewish people in admiring terms, gives me a sense of kinship. Yes, I believe I could tell them anything about myself or ask anything about themselves without embarrassment.

"I have a question for both of you," I say. "A high school teacher, a white woman, told me that when she asked her class recently if they have experienced prejudice in this school, a black boy said, 'Yes, the teachers always turn to me when anything about black people comes up and I don't like that.' Now here are teachers trying to create bridges and the opposite occurs. What's the answer?"

The Arnolds grin at each other. "We know how that boy feels," Mr. Arnold says. "It happens to us at professional meetings. But we must overcome this resistance. Who else can people ask about the black experience if not us? We can't say we're being ignored and then get annoyed when we're asked to talk about ourselves."

Mrs. Arnold waits for her husband to finish speaking, then adds, "It's hard for black kids with a white teacher. Maybe if the teachers begin real early in school getting *everyone* to talk about themselves the black children won't feel they're being singled out."

"I'm sure you're right. When I asked Mrs. Johnston to come in and tell us a story, her first question was, 'Are you inviting only the black parents?' I told her that the point was to include every family and she was relieved, I think."

"Now, about this high school student," Mr. Arnold says, "the one who objects to being spokesman for his people. The teacher can put the matter to the whole class. 'Okay, then what is the best way for me to get this sort of information without appearing racist?' Let everyone struggle with the problem."

*L*orraine immediately envisions the scene when I tell her about the high school boy who would not be questioned. "And the white teacher backed off, right? Most people will. Okay, here's what I think has to be said: Listen, there are some things I need to know. And I don't know who else to learn them from. Except you. Or from black colleagues and parents. And while none of us is an expert and we each have our own opinions, nevertheless that's the only way anyone is going to learn, by asking questions."

Her response is logical and fair but I wonder how many white teachers feel confident enough to follow Lorraine's example. The New Hampshire teacher who worries about singling out a black parent or child might need other experiences before she is ready to begin an open interrogation.

Lorraine seems to read my mind. "I know it's not easy. We need practice in asking people sensitive questions about themselves and, in turn, being asked about ourselves. But after a while, we are not afraid to ask. I'm getting this practice when I attend the people of color conferences."

"Is it very different," I ask, "when you and I talk together?"

"It really is, Vivian, when minority teachers tell their stories to each other. Some have horror tales, others relate wonderful experiences, and we identify with each speaker on an emotional level. We can give each other support and encouragement because we face so many of the same problems."

"Then what happens when you return to your white schools?"

"Well, I can tell you what happened to me," Lorraine answers. "I became willing to take more risks. I've been together with all those people of color who talk about taking a situation in their schools and changing it. Not only are we given specific ideas about how to make changes but we borrow from the strength it took to make the changes."

This is how I feel too, I want to tell Lorraine, after talking to her and to the black parents: a little stronger and willing to take more risks. Yet if I went to the people of color conference I'd be an outsider, just as Mrs. Arnold says she feels she is at our school.

"Let me give an example of how these conferences affect me," Lorraine continues. "There is one issue I've talked about here for many years, the idea of clustering black kids into relatively larger groups rather than spreading them out, a few in each class. Now, supposedly, our school is sympathetic to the concept and we've made significant progress. You have supported me on this, Vivian, and so have others. But there are still classrooms with just one black girl or boy. I've often thought, do I want to go on spinning my wheels on this subject? Then I hear minority teachers from all over the country discussing the same problem and my resolve is strengthened. Yes, I will keep repeating these ideas at faculty meetings, to the administration, and to individual teachers."

"Why do you think it's been such a struggle?"

"Oh, for a lot of good but, in my opinion, insufficient reasons. I'm told that if we cluster the black children it will result in classrooms with no black children at all. Then some white kids won't get to know black kids during that school year. However, the value of the black students' experience in a class with half a dozen or more other black children far outweighs any other consideration. Every minority teacher I've met agrees with me on this point. Look, you asked me the other day about kinship feelings. Well, they can't develop with minority children so fragmented in each class and with so few minority teachers."

"Lorraine, are you sure the black parents themselves won't object to your plan?"

"Many will, in fact. They may even see this as segregation. But we need to explain ourselves to all the parents. It's not only a black issue."

I wonder how often the high school boy who didn't want to talk sat in a classroom alone or perhaps with just one or two other black children. I understand the feelings of a white teacher who doesn't want to be deprived of black students, and yet, I am certain Lorraine is right. There should be a community, within the larger group, of people who look like each other and share a similar culture.

"Lorraine, Mrs. Arnold feels that African Americans have their own issues, not the same as other people of color. Do you sometimes feel this way at these conferences?"

"Sure I do, but there is strength in numbers. And all minorities have so much in common. We need to push the multicultural curriculum in all its variety and have more required reading by nonwhite authors on nonwhite themes. We talk about this all the time."

As we begin to collect our things, I am suddenly aware that there are many questions I have not yet asked. The school year is almost over; this may be our last "official" conversation. "Lorraine," I ask, "when you were a child how did you feel about having been descended from slaves?"

She always makes me feel my questions are neither unexpected nor out of place. "I can't tell you the extreme embarrassment I suffered. Even though my childhood was spent with black people in a wonderful community, the very thought of slavery was a humiliation. But my parents told me, 'You're not the one who should be embarrassed. The people who enslaved us need to be embarrassed. They're the ones who did a wrong. We didn't do a wrong.'"

"Do black children still feel embarrassed?"

"There is more anger now. So maybe they have put the blame where it belongs. But there is also curiosity and a sense of pride. African Americans spend a lot of time tracing family trees. There are all kinds of courses at the DuSable Museum. People sometimes even find a bill of sale and they can pinpoint what country in Africa they come from. This is a big activity among the blacks and it's a boon to the children."

As we walk down the hall, I blurt out a final question. "What do you think is the value of this book I'm writing? You've read parts of the manuscript, mainly to see if I'm quoting you properly. But you've never told me how you feel about it."

Lorraine stops and turns to me. "It's all about dialogue, isn't it? To me, colleagues can read your book and see that they can sit down and talk to each other and to the parents. And parents can read the book and see that it is a good thing to talk to the teachers. You are encouraging the dialogue, not necessarily the answers, but the dialogue. This points to the need for more people of color in the schools. So there can *be* the dialogue."

This kind of communication has no end and there is always another story to be told.

"Once there was a princess who talked only Spanish," Kesha dictates at the story table.

"Is she the same princess you told us about a long time ago?" I ask.

"No, this princess is a brown girl. Her name is Annabella. And this princess could talk any language. When she talked Indian she was Indian and when she talked—what does Nada in the first grade talk?"

"Polish."

"Oh, yeah. When she talked Polish she was Polish and when she talked every language she was every person. So she lived happily ever after."

"How could she know all the languages?" Martha asks.

"Because she asked everyone to teach her."